The raising light trilogy

Mike Johnson

Press

99% Press,
an imprint of Lasavia Publishing Ltd.
Auckland, New Zealand

www.lasaviapublishing.com

ISBN: 978-0-9951282-3-1

For Leila Lees and the family:
Paul, Paloma, Rowan and Sophia

Author's note

I was half way through writing the second volume in this trilogy before I realized that the three books were a unity, beginning with the fascinations of childhood in Toybox, through the searching and yearning of maturity in Hide your Eyes – The Rumi Poems, to an unwilling confrontation with the end in Extinction Rebellion – A Tribute. Each book has been published as a separate volume.

This book would not look as wonderful as it does without the cover artwork of Leila Lees, the cover design by Jennifer Rackham, the layout and book design by Daniela Gast and the proofreading of Neil Sonnekus and Janscie Sharplin. I am lucky to have such a team.

Contents

The Toy Box 7

Hide Your Eyes – The Rumi Poems 123

EXTINCTION REBELLION – A TRIBUTE 241

Book One

The Toy Box

The Soul

In Queen Street
on Friday night
– lights blooming but
already pomegranate-heavy
with Adult Entertainment –
a yellow balloon
was hopping around
among herds of cars,
holding its helium soul together,
two lives left,
to the music of singing ironclads,
hopping, filled with its yellow
balloon-fright
before wheels
and behind wheels
incapable of salvation
incapable of destruction,
one life left,
half a life left,
with a molecular trace of helium,

using its last resources
its string searching
for some child's hands
Sunday morning

Miroslav Holub

Translated by Dana Hábová
And David Young

Into the Toy Box

Part One

the first page

the first page opens
a staircase
into the
turning world
of the toy box
with all its bits and bobs
and happenstance

toys that sit
toys that don't
pieces that fit
pieces that won't
and pieces that belong
to quite another puzzle

there goes Jack Horner and Little Boy Blue
across the gutter and
around the corner of the illustration
into the everyday street
where everyone walks
spits their hopes and fears
and buys toys for the kids
at that time of the year

they look the same
as everybody else with somewhere to go
even if it's let's-pretend
and there's lots of let's-pretend
to go around

walk for long enough and you will find Margery Door
still on her see-saw, Mother Goose amid
gigabytes of mountains and imaginations
and you might like to grab
a quick snack with the Muffin Man
down in Drury Lane

a nice way to finish the day
in toy land

you can see all this stuff as the morning grows
easy as turning a new leaf
opening a vein
or wandering in the forever afternoon, climbing the
Faraway Tree, trying not to wonder why
as the shadows climb up after you
anyone would want to bake
four-and-twenty blackbirds in their feathers
still dreaming of flightless skies

a house with no windows

they made a house out of bricks and sand
and sticky stuff
but forgot to put in the windows

the man in the moon was sad
because he had no nice glass to shine through

so he went to ask the jade rabbit
who'd been digging holes in the moon
for all eternity (it's easy to see them!)
to ask for advice

you can't ask me, the rabbit said, because
I dig burrows and burrows don't have
windows, silly – deep underground there is a burrow
heaven
and it has no windows

so the man in the moon visited the woodcutter
who worked alone in the dark, cutting down
an acacia tree, which healed itself
after every blow of his silver axe

you can't ask me, the woodcutter said
I have no time, I'm too busy to look around
and can only see your light
in the blade of my axe

so the man in the moon went to the goddess who lives
in the mountains of the moon
in a splendid palace of ice

you can't ask me, she said, I've been
banished from the earth forever
because I stole my king's elixir
and so a house without windows
is just like my heart, all closed off
and shut away

this made the man in the moon even sadder:
        he couldn't shine in the rabbit's burrow
        he could only shine on the woodcutter's blade
        he couldn't shine in the goddess's heart
        he couldn't even shine on the foolish toys
who forgot to put windows in their houses
of bricks and sand and sticky stuff

but there was love in his heart, even for the poor
chipped and broken toys with their eyes rubbed out

and their houses with no windows, no doors even,
so he turned his sad face away, to the other side, the dark side
where the stars alone could see his tears
and his bright and happy face might always
be looking our way

the story bag

it’s a cloth bag
drawn tight with a blue drawstring
heavy with stories
all in different shapes
weights and colours

the word made flesh
the flesh made word
the word made king
the king made queen
and everything between

stories for all ages and rages
from pins to pumpkins
from cats to cages
snake and fox

stories of loss and of gain
whole or in part
old or fresh

here’s a piece of jade
that fell from the moon

still glowing
and turned the sea green

here's pearl of ancient rain
locked in swamp gum

this one is a starfish
a long way from memories of the sea
and the circular swing of the galaxy

this one a ceramic blowfish
that doubles as a whistle
(you blow through the tail)

and here's a piece of plaid
paper thin, with a yellowy look
your grandmother must have added
as a little domestic touch

plus one bird's nest
in a green flame

and here's a seed
from deep space, reddy-brown
shaped like a heart

some are warm to the touch
some have faces
some are lost in time
some spurn love, some seek fame

some hide away in shame
and some build houses
and some tear them down

some are, probably,
most decidedly, not true
while others make their own
arrangements with verisimilitude

it's a lot for a little cloth bag
drawn tight with a blue drawstring
a lot of whispering
in even the darkest of places

stories spilling out
into the toy box

the truth about the rescue of the story bag

Anansi
the floppy spider with green eyes,
spun a thread to heaven
to rescue the story bag
from the fearsome sky god
Nyame
who had taken all the stories of the world
for himself
to have and to hoard
forever and a day

humanity had grown sad
without its stories; children
couldn't sleep at night, the stars
forgot to shine
and even dogs lost
their bone-hill dreams

nobody knew where to go
or what to do
or even why they should
get up in the morning

or go to bed at night
it was as if all the stories of the world
had died
and left no marker of their passing

Nyame set Anansi three impossible tasks
but spidy would have none of that

he'd heard of those kinds of deals before
the story bag was full of them
dangerous situations
heroics required in every case
along with wit, wisdom
and dedication

where truth lies
stories too are spun like silken threads
from the inflated fantasies
of clever, trickier gods

but the truthful truth is that Anansi
got Nyame drunk with a special potion
containing spider venom
which caused his majesty to fall in love

with his second cousin
and in the confusion Anansi stole
the story bag and spiralled back to earth
with all the stories of the world

safe and sound
even this one
for the special enjoyment of our ears
our ears, our ears

Scheheraza de: a still life

the picture shows
a young woman on an embroidered cushion
sitting in front of her king

she looks very composed

the king lounges back, one knee up
an arm resting loosely upon it
the other hand holding a hookah
from which there arise spirals and
curlicues and fairy rings

in the background attendants hover

by his side a scimitar
with a curved moon blade
and an ornate guard
lies negligently
on the folds of his royal gown

the king looks very composed
the hookah looks very dignified
the spirals and curlicues and fairy rings

are fantastical
the attendants are suitably awed

and the scimitar looks as if it were dreaming
perhaps of a red satin cushion
in a palace of peace
with the burbling call of doves
and the quiver of water in cool stone pools
where rainbow coloured fish flick
from instant to instant

she is leaning forwards, one hand raised flat
palm up
as if she were offering him a delicacy
on a plate, her head tilted up a little
her mouth open

words! I know she needs words
I would love to help her with some
words love to be needed
or they go brown and die like fallen leaves

but it's more than words she needs
it's a special magic, a story magic
as each word awaits the next
most breathlessly
and events can hardly keep pace

with themselves
meanwhile, the king keeps smoking his hookah
with spirals and curlicues and fairy rings

the attendants hover expectantly

and the scimitar keeps dreaming
of vanquished foes,
of an exalted future in the Hand of God
as the greatest sword of all time
with the sharpest blade of all time
the sword of swords

a proud blade that would never
stoop to beheading a girl like this
this particular girl, in fact
who speaks so sweetly, whose only crime
is innocence
and to have to feel once more
sticky human blood along the blade

the picture shows
a scene of opulent tranquility
but everybody knows
even the gloating attendants

where the story must end

the pop-up ballerina

the music box hasn't been opened
for a very long time
its hinges are stiff

the pop-up ballerina
has had no chance to pop up
and whirl around
to a tinkle-dinkle version
of twinkle-twinkle little star
or Fűr Elise
or Chopin's Nocturne

no chance to captivate
even for a moment
with visions of impossible purity
and rinky-dink sweetness
the sunlit nursery
the moonlit nursery
the moment of magic in the toy box
the suspension of disbelief
when imaginings become plangent
the pace brisk
before the slow winding down

plink by
plonk

the long wait for the next note
the final moment of incredulity
when everything stops

the music box hasn't been opened
since the last nostalgic moment
and nobody knows if the music still plays
or if the ballerina will appear
and make a comeback
but everyone is keeping fingers crossed
for in that moment, that silly pink
and twirly moment
we might be ourselves, as at the very first
when the spring is wound up
tight
the tune fresh
and the ballerina takes the stage

narratives on the run

1

one fine day
(in the middle of the night)
they loosened the drawstring and
out of the story bag they came
all in a rush
narratives on the loose
impatient
bursting with words
leaping into what they hoped
was the bright light
or any kind of light
leaving the old and the tired dark
behind

there isn't a narrative that doesn't dream
of freedom
in its heart of hearts

but it was kind of crowded and dim
in the toy box
with so many soft-machine dreams
jostling around

that the stories had nowhere much to go
no secure place
no cyber-protected soapbox
no home in the eye of a friendly reader
and nobody much to admire them

so they took to the four directions
heedless
and in search of true gods
and divine fonts

2

it wasn't long before Anansi gave the alarm
and the hunt was on
hither and yon, high and low
here and beyond the lexicon and the
phonemes of desire

even the humans joined in
the little girl in red gumboots
with some of the bolder toys
Big Ted and Little Ed
Noddy, and the girls from the cowboy band
searched together all around

here and there, under the sofa
behind the fridge
on top of old smoky
beside running waters
and the inside of buckets with crenellations
for making sand castles
you never know where a story might hide
or syllables stashed

the stories were not to be found
neither within nor without
above or below
and a great wordless wailing shook the world

perhaps the skygod has come down
from his lofty heights
and stolen the stories from
under our tongues again
people said

they searched under their tongues
interrogated their voice boxes
squeezed their lungs
and made a great fuss before heaven

turned the toy box upside down
and shook the world from side to side

before everyone got seasick

3

from the stories' point of view
being out of the bag was not all
it was cracked up to be
there were no cheering crowds
no laurels to wear or sit on
no handsome volumes seeking them out
no handmade paper, with marbled end-pages
and crafted leather spines
awaited their pleasure

it was dusty under the sofa
it was cramped behind the fridge
and all the other places had problems
problems! problems!
it was no better in the kitchen
behind the pots and pans
or in the great metaphysical beyond
where abstractions ruled
and narratives pined away

some became so depressed
they lost their cutting edge
or devised gloomy endings

no reader would care to stomach
others had grimmer fates
still others dreamed of dissolving
back into the Great Dictionary
in the hope of being reborn again
sometime

eventually peace was declared, since stories
are made for ears, big and little
flesh and fabric, plain or plastic
there is no better place
to rehearse their lines
than the nice, snug, welcoming
story bag

Noddy – a short story

not fair to say that Noddy is the dumbarse of Toy
Town
although his bell does a fair amount of jingling
on top of his spring-loaded head
to little effect

and he is a tad too easily frightened

Big Ears too has come under a lot of flack
for being a hearty know-nothing
with an overfondness for platitudes
and a suspicious attachment
to the little wooden toy with the dunce's hat
the painted smile
and the helpless noddy-nod-nod of his little head

those toy-town gossips will never understand
the true nature of bromance

in fact, everybody takes care of the little
nodding man – he never comes to any harm –
and Mr Plod, a cop of immeasurable slowness
of speech, always remembers what Noddy's house

looks like even when Noddy himself
has forgotten

once he went to Big Ears' house thinking
that he was Big Ears
they had a lot of muddily sorting out to do
after which they sat down for a nice cup of tea

not the squarest block in the box, but getting there
and look, he has his own little yellow car with the
blue fenders, he's coming along just fine
is Noddy
thank you very much
and never forget that, like you and me
and everybody else in the box,
he too was made by Old Man Carver

the tale of Wee Ted and the pumpkin seeds

it was all the doing of the littlest toy
in the box – Wee Ted
(with the smallest bed)
who set out
searching for the beans
that might float him all the way up
to the land of the big people
where Old Man Carver lives
and as every toy knows, Old Man Carver
is the author of many a rocking horse
and every little wooden toy from here
to kingdom come

now Wee Ted was none too smart
his head was made of soft stuff
his limbs were even softer
while his eyes were crosses of black thread
frayed

he wasn't much good outside the toy box
thinking the floor was the ceiling
the ceiling was the walls

and walls were some impossible
horizon line

that windows were square moons
and that Old Man Carver might live on top
of the kitchen table or in the linen cupboard

and nothing had prepared him for real mice

he found his magic beans which of course
were not beans but who's to say - if Wee Ted
thinks they're beans then they have
a fair chance of being beans
despite their determined pumpkinness
their shape and smell

beaniness is in the eye of the beholder
in this case a button eye

they may not put down roots into the dust
at the bottom of the toy box
or scale the heights of air to the land
of the big people
but they are just great at playing let's pretend
with the littlest toy in the box
and even a pumpkin might one day
turn into a magic bean
and grow and grow
and grow

the colouring book

the colouring-in book remains
mostly uncoloured
with a few zig-zag crayon marks
at random
and occasionally
a green or yellow head
or lavender shoes
or a dog with a blue tongue
or dirty marks where little fingers tried
to claw out the sun

there's a pig with spectacles
reading *The Times*
with red blobs for hands
Sunday blue for eyes not quite fixed
in their frame
and a golden arrow
where his heart should be

there's Mary Mouse with her broom
tackling armies of dust, the broom
having got ahead of itself, its own
purple patch yet to be swept

has been cancelled by some black crosses
running from gutter to corner
never intended to colour anything

she's an extreme case

Mr Plod blowing his whistle
under a crayon-bruised sky
has a touch of orange on each knee
and his face has been reshaped
to look like a pumpkin
with mauve dots
and an amber antenna
a Plod from outer space

some serious intent here

and so it goes for every page
you'll have to look for yourself
if you want more of the same
page after page
hectically turned with a few
rubs and slashes and furry balls
looks like it was all used up

in a single day

a single hour
its cover now torn
pages stuck together
by lumps of coloured grease
not quite ready for the scrap heap

not quite used up, it remains
misused

a wasted world of black lines
some capricious god
could never bring into being
or quite believe in
but could happily scribble over

the fork and spoon tango

when the fork ran away with the spoon
there was a great ta-doo in the toy box

you can read all about in the *Fairy Tale Times*

the truth is that nobody sang
hey diddle diddle (as if they would!)
the little dog did not laugh
to see such craft, the notion of a cow
jumping over the moon
was patently ridiculous
and the cat and the fiddle
would have nothing to do with it
full stop

shame on the FTT for spreading
false news stories, and hyping
what was a most personal
and painful matter, an unlikely love affair
of the most haunting kind

the disappearance of the fork and the spoon
is that much more mysterious

given their mutual embarrassment
on discovering
that they were in love
and no amount of rattling of the cutlery drawer
would change that

in the normal world forks want to fork
and spoons want to spoon
and in this way the natural order is maintained
but when the world gets turned over
and inside out
by love
a fork may want to spoon
and a spoon may want to fork
without rhyme or reason
so who are we to mock
or question
the great spoonfork
of the universe
which may burst in upon us
in our forkedness and spoonness
and send us
scratching against the walls of the toy box

the FTT's fanciful little tale
might be fine for children to sing

and perhaps no one has to know
the tragedy lurking in the ditty
the humiliation of the hey diddle diddle
or has to wonder
what became of them
if they are clinking together
somewhere
or are far far far
far apart

a good old sing-song

once a month or so
everybody stands around the piano
and has a good old sing-song
just like the old days

dressed in their Sunday best
the toys come
and if they don't remember all the words
it doesn't matter
because someone else does
and as long as they all sway
back and forward in the same direction
everything goes pretty well

their voices will never soar to heaven
on the back of a descant
nor set the body quivering
with a touch of fire – Big Ted
looks as if he might be courting a stroke
with his mouth open and his face purple
but he's not one to shun the high notes
and Wee Ted will roll over backwards
to hit the bass

it's a bit like being in church except
you're allowed to laugh
when a note comes out wrong
or a word is forgotten
or a phrase misplaced
because of a lifetime spent not singing

the piano has seen better days
but so has everybody
so nobody cares too much
it doesn't so much play the notes
(which don't sound quite right)
as remember them from the honky-tonk
barroom years when the keys were called
ivories and the sounds held true
right to the dying fall
of sackcloth and sad songs
wars and reunions
loves and lost loves and loves
that never were

a lot of loves went marching off in a major key
while the minor keys stayed at home weeping
but the toys knew none of this
even those who sang the loudest
or with the most feeling

and the words… the words…
well the words are just something to sing
around the piano
after all

the little tractor

the little tractor has something wrong
with its wind-up heart

it went into stop-go mode
then stopped altogether

once it had some pretty fine action
whirring over a ploughed carpet
or chugging up the armrest of a settee
all by itself

a certain integrity of intention
you might say, a bit of the toughness
you might expect
from a little motor made to be tough
just like the big ones

some say its cogs got all graunched
so it couldn't be wound up
while others say that someone
lost the key
that's all
while still others maintain

it hit the wall
and its wheels kept grinding away
until it gave up hope

and now its wheels won't even turn

one day a child, a notional child,
will pick it up and skim it or grind it
over the carpet
but it won't be the same
only any good in fantasy land
where the child has to make
the *grum-grum* sound
any proud motor would make
given half a chance

the little tractor has something wrong
with its wind-up heart
and already it can feel the rust
corroding
its once mighty spring

visit the gift horse

don't pause to count the teeth
in the mouth of a gift horse
they say
among other things they say

there's a gift horse in the toy box
that will make your every wish come true
if you wish for it hard enough
they say

a sort of resident genie
in disguise
an ordinary enough looking gift horse
made of soft green stuff with a nice red coat
and proper ears sewn on
and a red mouth to match the coat
probably not many teeth
one doesn't like to ask
or look too hard

but this ordinary looking toy
has extraordinary gifts, beyond counting
beyond your wildest dreams

beyond all there is and will be
the gifts that go on giving
unheralded and unsung

if
you would like to see a place
where the rich are made poor
and the poor can eat
and a mountain can float free
of the encumbrance of the earth
and all that is sick is made well
and all that is well is made divine
heart, blood and blood cell
and you don't have to worry
about what might happen if you get your wish
then
visit the gift horse
bearing your life in your hands like a beach ball
you can drop
and make your wish right there

and this little gift horse will get
right to work, changing the universe around
to suit your wishes, upending old regimes
and bringing in the wind
sorting out time and sequence

to make sense to the eye
and bringing some brave love
in from the cold
don't look a gift horse in the mouth
teeth or no teeth
they say
among other things they say

and there is wisdom in that
for the gift horse only comes around
once in a blue moon
with his fine red coat
and his sewn-on ears
and the power to move worlds

a place in the scheme of things

the Jack of Spades endures
its separation from the pack
with a stoical mien

desertion, abandonment, loss
absence from the hierarchy of meanings
or the order of angels
it regards with aplomb

loss of family and friends, rivals
and lovers
is harder to take
but who's counting?

fondly it remembers life on the shuffle
with all its cuzzie bros and colleagues
teasers and leavers
its place in the scheme of things
its skin in the game

it would no more
defy the ace than despise the ten
for it has no need

to reassure itself that the
mighty Jack of Spades

is just the card to be
when the chips are down

for in the fall of the cards it might find
the power of the bower
outrank even the cunning ace
turn a losing hand into a winning one
or complete a straight or flush

the One Eyed Jack, they call it
because the other eye is looking out into
another universe
no gambler can see
and dreams of plays no earthly player
can execute

we have to ask what it's doing
on the bottom of the toy box
face down
alone
nothing but the other eye
to see with

maybe the whole pack is scattered
to the four winds
the Jack the last left standing
against all odds

waiting for the game to resume
to be picked
and carefully positioned
to be loved again
to feel the weight of a greater fate

in some new game of chance

no stay of execution for the ditherers

in Toy Town
the jug is always full
but the bench is mostly empty
and everybody has either gone home
or yet to arrive

there's little room
for half-measures
or fuzzy in-betweens
false reassurances
or delayed effects

the jug is always empty
but the bench is mostly full
everybody has already arrived
or gone shopping

the jug sits upside down
on the table – nobody gets wet
nobody says anything that shouldn't be said
nothing has to be taken back
brought forward

or tabled for a vote
jug and bench make a perfect pair
one full, the other empty, one empty
the other full
they swap yarns on a Saturday night
and remember what the other forgets
which is a great way to do it
no questions asked
and nobody has to tell any lies

it's like that everywhere, the same jug
the same bench
the same eternal arrangement
people coming and going
threading
present and past
idea and form
time and circumstance

when all ambiguity is banished
the 'neither here nor there' crowd
get a short shrift

no stay of execution
for the ditherers
the fence sitters

the dollar-each-way crowd
jug and bench are empty and full
the people are alive or dead
god doesn’t hesitate
Toy Town always gets its just deserts
one way or the other

the great leveler

it was a set-up from the start
the dolls were all lined up
their dresses crisp
their smiles identical
their deception immaculate
their price tags carefully hidden
unless on special

freshly unwrapped, cleared
of its cellophane cowl
the doll steps forward in all its glory
plastic hair gleaming
not a mark or scratch
the delicious smell of plastic
fresh off the assembly line

the clothes too, suitable
as evening wear, a cocktail party
or a restaurant where the waiters
wear bow ties
modest but classy
without a smudge or crinkle
there is nothing like

that first pristine moment
before anything happens

and destiny and fate and all
the other pretenders
throw their hats into the ring

of course you and I know that
without fail
the joy will wear off
the sequins will lose their glitter
and no matter how glad the rags
how grandiose the visions
or impeccable the pedigree
it's all pretty much the same
after a while

in the toy box

Goldilocks the refugee

she was little and sad and lost
had no home under the sun
and she'd come a long way
over some hard roads

perhaps she'd been cursed by a wicked fairy
or born to war and strife
in some place where it got too hot
and the rivers ran dry

there was dust on her dress,
her ankles were sore
and when a door opened up in a world
with the light too bright
she had no choice but to step through
into the cool interior
the shady spaces
of somebody else's home

the interloper

knowing
if she kept trying, there was a place

just for her, a world that fitted her
a place to eat and sleep

and dream, not of dog-faced soldiers
or burnt meadows
but a little house, in a wood
near a green, by rushing water
with a kindly teddy bear
watching over her sleep

that useless plastic tree

we'd agree
that a tiny plastic tree
like this one
is not much use to anybody
but for the most fleeting of attention
from some toddler
who's not fooled anyway
and is fast learning the difference
between things you can eat
and things you might choke on

yet there it is at the bottom of the toy box
more plastic than tree, so carelessly shaped
no particular tree springs to mind
just the most basic generic form
no attempt at branches, and
with little flaps of plastic left over
from the pressing

if you broke it in half
it wouldn't bleed
its base is so malformed
it will barely stand
but once it was placed somewhere

to lord it over an imaginary forest
full of lyrical, magical things
or mark a fancy boulevard
fit for kings or queens
in the tinpot dreams of Toy Town

now it's gathering dust
a useless hunk of junk
destined for some landfill
or some ocean – did it give
a moment's pleasure, could it ever
forget its rigid plasticness
its lumpish tragedy

its worse-than-uselessness?

they dance before the faithless

these little red shoes took her feet
on a merry dance
until her feet were gone
and even that couldn't stop them

feet or no feet
the dance goes on

laughter in the ballroom
songs in the meadows
weeping in the forest

the executioner lined up her legs
decided to chop her off at the knees
to make her more acceptable

for his sword he chose
the edge of the gibbous moon
a slice of darkness

she said her farewells
and bled into the stars

the little red shoes
still haunt the church
and dance before the faithless
most prettily

feet or no feet
girl or no girl
the dance goes on

prayers in the vestry
dirges in the meadows
arias on the bridges

you can hear the tap-tap-tapping
of the obscene rhymes, and the cries
of the orphans and their children
as counterpoint, contrapuntal

none have penetrated
to the secret heart of the girl
who couldn't stop dancing

the big bad wind blew into town

Toy Town clock tower
got knocked over by a big bad wind
nobody knew whether to laugh or cry
or just fall down

now time has lost its way
in the dark-dark woods
with no crumbs or white stones
to follow

the clock tower was never
much to write home about
it never aspired to touch
the hem of heaven
or become a beacon of hope
was never much use for anything
but for climbing up and down
the way the ants did
and it didn't offer much of a view
beyond the rim of the toy box

it would never have won
an architectural award

not even in the land of toys
where tottering towers teetered

on a regular basis
and the impermanence of all things
ruled

the big bad wind – that was something else
it didn't belong in the land of toys
it had no place in the story bag
it was never sewn into flags
or left behind in the dreamcatcher

it blew in from some other place

yet it woke the child
with the fall of a lonesome train whistle
disturbed the dreams of the dreamers
with the sound of giant footfalls
and a dire song
about the end of time

some saw it as a portent
some as an act of dog
some as a game of numbers
some as a joke

and some saw it
as way beyond the joke

but whatever it was or did or meant
it knocked down that little clock
tower
that had never done any harm

now time lies on its side
general confusion reigns
as everybody forgets what time it is
what day it is
and when they might die

and then the wicked fairy came

someone has cast a spell on the toy box
things ain't what they used to be

once there was lots of hurrying and scurrying
to-ing and fro-ing, and everybody was busy
keeping busy with something
important

if it weren't for all this keeping busy
there'd be nothing to do

Mrs Broom swept clean
Mr Brush swept dirty
in the children's room, the dance
of the feather duster and the fly swat
kept things lively
kept the dust on the move
and the smile on the face
of the smiley face

while the little electric engine that could
went around and around and aroundabout
and lost the four directions as east went west

and north went south
but nobody cared too much, hell,
it was party time even in the dark-dark woods
where the goblins live

then the wicked fairy came
if that's what it was
like a thief in the night
and touched the sky
and even the earth, and shook
all the creatures that live on the earth
even all the creepy-crawlies

and all those that were touched
lost themselves
and no longer knew the toy box
for what it was

now they look like they're moving
but they're only playing let's pretend
the hare and the bear sit down for tea
with buttons for scones
(one for you and two for me)
and laces for graces
but they're only playing let's pretend

Noddy and Big Ears go for a walk
have a little talk but nothing gets said
no words are spoken
because they're only playing let's pretend
things have never been the same
since the wicked fairy came
and cast its horrid spell

I wish I wish I wish
I could tell them
no spell lasts forever, friends
comrades of the toy box!
we have magicians working overtime
on the problem
and Mighty Mouse in the wings
always ready… steady
here I come to save the day!

where it goes, nobody knows

time's not the same in the toy box
it's more like playdough
or that gooey stuff you throw at walls
and it sticks… for a while

it can get a bit spooky
at night in the toy box
with nothing to comfort you
but the muddledy dreams of Raggedy Ann
in which time does a loop-de-loop
and comes back as the enemy
the steady march of the clock-tick

meanwhile some of the smarter toys
like Jiminy Cricket
have begun to suspect
that they are losing pieces of time
as surely as they are losing their stuffing
or the colour
off their once shiny paint jobs

but where time flows, nobody knows
and nobody knows how far it goes
or where it stops

time flakes off, the cricket said
and Pooh Bear agrees – he's seen
some pretty flaky time in his time
'not every pot of honey is equal in weight'
he says
which is really wise
for a bear of very little brain

Bob the Builder and the Bobsy Twins
wake up in a place where no time passes
everything hangs suspended
the clock stops, never to go again

the arrow at the bottom of the box
is frozen in mid-air, no nearer, no further away
from the target
which is nothing more than a face
in the hallows of memory

it's true, time is not the same in the toy box
it's gone all corkscrew
and put the toys into a coma

you'll know what's happened if you stare hard
enough
into their blank faces
and listen for their absent whispers
in their world of lost words

no place for realism

in the toy box there is no birth
or death
although things do fall apart
and new things might arrive
fully made
at my given moment
out of nowhere

nobody has any babies
but there's lots of pretending
like Mrs Weathervane and her pram
or Peta Peatwater with her plastic womb
but smooth between the legs

the toy box is no place for realism
some details are best skipped over
imagination is required to turn
plastic into flesh and a hollow place
or stuffed space
into blood and bone

there may be a train station

or a police box, or a house
made out of blocks
but you won't see a funeral parlour

or a cemetery
because the area is strictly patrolled
by lead soldiers with muskets
brightly painted
whose job it is
to keep the outside separated from
the inside, and the above separated
from the below
so everybody can sleep happily at night
without having to worry

besides, friends, it's amazing what you
can patch up and cobble together
with a little needle and thread
not quite as grandiose as birth and death
perhaps
but it does the job
and gives some old comrades
a new lease of life

now you see me

the dreams of the toy box
are all of other places
far away from the paint-scratched
mishmash
of some very untidy toys

there are lots of clean white lines
and children-free spaces
lovely zen silences
and a somewhere over the rainbow

as well as beaches and beach balls
and cheeks as rosy as
and sunlit spaces
and plenty of places to play
now-you-see-me-now-you-don't
or
catch-me-if-you-can

there're hills too, real ones
with yellow tussock that holds fast
to the rocky ground
and mountains that creak and tremble

when the sky comes too close to dreams
and trucks that ruck and rumble
all the way into playtime

there are lots of big wide wonderful
open landscapes to run around in
and trees to climb with real branches
that break if you go too high
and real streams for pretend boats
and real birds to peck out your eyes
and a real meal on the table

the dreams of the toy box are not
of the toy box but very far away
as far as myth and makeshift will go
as far as memory and imagination
even to the edge of the great ocean
so great it has no horizon
and I would beware, if I were you
of loose talk about kapok dreams
or plastic dreams
or wooden dreams
or feather dreams
or the metal dreams
of tin soldiers

bashed, dented, kicked, chewed
and regularly upended
the pristine dreams of the toy box
become all we remember
and are

a troubling poignancy

toys will dream
that one day they will lose
their toyness
and turn into real little children
with inaugurations all their own

it is a desire filled with a troubling
poignancy
a disturbing sense of not belonging
of not being as real as everything else
of rejection and abandonment

of course toys don't think
about such things
overtly
or even feel such things
covertly
but
being made of wood and plastic and fluff
doesn't mean a toy can't
wake up with a peculiar pain
in the heart
or a memory that can be traced back

to before the invention of stars
or the writing of texts

I don't think the toys really want
to be actual children
they couldn't bear it

but in their dreams they take flesh
and like kings and queens
feel the sun on their faces
that won't blister their paint
and grow legs that can walk them
through gardens of scented delight

on vesper wings
they go
with no one to see them or remind them
that they are, after all,
only toys
with nothing but toy dreams

the harlequin's farewell party

the toys hold a farewell party
for one leaving the toy box and the pages
of fairy tales
for parts unknown
and adventures inconceivable

the children call it growing up
but of course toys don't grow up, do they?
they only pretend

take Noddy for example – first he was alone
in the dark-dark wood, then Big Ears found him
and since then nothing has changed
he is not just passing through, he is home
under a big never-changing ceiling
with only groundless fears to face

not so the harlequin
with his brightly patched coat
his shredded trews, his bells
and his bare feet
the harlequin has places to go,
people to see

deals to make, vistas to take in
nightmares to ride out

he isn't the type to get stuck in the toy box
forever and a day
riding the little engine that could around and around
seeing the same faces
day in day out
night in night out
until hell freezes over

the hobo steps to the road
heads for new climes
beyond the table leg,
beyond the clatter and the natter
beyond the edge of the door
beyond the edge of sunlight
where the gingerbread man runs
over the hill and far away
up the road and around the bend
neither envied nor remembered
which is how he likes it

in the world but not of it
everywhere and nowhere
the one that got away

you can't say we didn't get fair warning

when the lights are switched off
a glow still filters under the door
just enough to show something
but not enough to show anything

there's only so far you can go
to keep your promises
keep your head above water
show enough but not too much
just enough but not too little

there's only so far you can go
to keep your end of the bargain
to hold it in your heart
to keep it dear to you, like a shrine
to keep it out of the shadows
to keep it where you can see it
to know its partial revelation
like the time in the garden with
the sunwine
and the starwine
and the crispy chips

you can't say we didn't get fair warning
when the light is switched off
what filters under the door is barely enough
to shape the body, desire, hope,
all that Mr Moonlight might bring
on the tripwires of memory

and no matter how far you go
it can never be far enough
from intruders who lurk
beyond the doorway
waiting for you
you who are standing by the toy box
in the half world

waiting

Out of the Toybox

Part Two

a big backyard

the child peeps
over the rim of the world

wonders await the eye
fulfilment awaits the heart

oh! here are stars that are not
sewn into silk

a moon and sun that are not
painted onto mirrors

people who walk and talk
whose feet move by themselves

and who have large voices freighting
carriages of air

here are windows to the soul
and other places

a big backyard
full of galaxies and radio stars

just beyond the fantasies of
the toy-box child

with his wooden knuckles
and wild, sapphire eyes

these adventures need you

time to set off for
high adventure, tales of the wicked
and derring-do
whether in a pea-green boat
hurled from sea to sea
riding a unicorn with an
iridescent horn
or flashing across spacetime
and other impossible places
in a craft of fine design
the aim is the same
the name of the game doesn't change
in love or war
and the stakes are staggeringly high

heroes are needed
to right the wrongs
to restore
the moral balance of the cosmos
and pluck armageddon
from the jaws of prophesy

it's an old story, always new

as are old lies, always true
and to the hero come the spoils

the rights to all the songs
and other ephemera

mountains high and valleys low
hobgoblins tall or squat
trolls at the bridge singing
foldewol foldewol
I'm a troll, I'm a troll
with the winter steps of memory
and everything held fragile in a breath
or left behind in the wreckage

the call to adventure
comes dressed in pyjamas
yet cloaked as destiny, heralded by
the cry of a crow or a diamond flash
on a dark horizon – gird yourself, pilgrim
and move out, time is antipathy
and rust never weeps

your loved ones will still be loved
and your grave ones will still be grave
that which is left behind would have beenleft behind

anyway
in the long run
that which is in front of you

will come in its own good time
when you will be called upon
to show your mettle
put your life on the line
and bend your head before
the fiery touch of some god or other

time to set out, time to sing the road
fling the wind
adventure doesn't linger for the timid
but chooses the boldest heroes
the most resolute
for the sacred task at hand

is that you or have we got it wrong?

the map is not the territory

the island is limned in black
a shadow image, a history

at first sight, you can't tell what it is
an ink splotch or a rocky dragon
hard to see it as a place where people live
and children play
and the world can seem close
or very far away

I love those old celluloid photos
the tight rolls of negatives
which would unwind
a world full of ghosts
with holes for eyes and bright silver hair

who might or might not have been family

we have these things

we have a beach a sky and garden
a dolls' house
a pretty, vacant space
all anybody could ask
sky-latched, tide-patched, earth-matched
memories patched, most not worth the time
spent making them in the first place

I might just as well have
stayed at home, sailed the winds on a lily
read a book in the panther hours
or whiled away my time in the toy box
between here and let's pretend
with my friends
and pat-a-cake some happy words
pat-a-cake pat-a-cake...

sometimes all anybody could ask
is not enough

I don't complain, I say to people,
but that's a lie – I complain all the time
about this and that and the great injustice of things

the beach salts over,the sky cracks open
the garden floods, the doll's house
gets stolen, the pretty space
crashes
somebody takes a poke at somebody
who passes it on
the toy box fills up with good wishes
as the purse empties

this has to be about as good as it gets

my dad would say

the street scene opens up like most street scenes
cars moving, people walking, shop windows gleam-
ing
words scurrying
all the wind-up toys toddling off home
or catching a train to Toy Town

he's got his head screwed on right
my dad would say
I tried to picture it, reconstruct it,
a whole world built
by men with their heads screwed on right
some with springs, some with cogs
some with bolts and some with braces
and some just stuffed with kapok

the cars stopped moving, the people stopped walking
the shop windows turned to dark glass
and time turned to super glue
at the checkout counter

then the street tipped at some fantastic angle, like
a ship sinking,

bringing the sky and the clouds down
to live among us
while worlds flashed and twinkled in our
well screwed on heads

sister sun and brother moon

side by side they sit
on a mossy wall long forgotten
to listen to the ocean
watch for signs of life, and stare
at the long horizon

sister sun and brother moon
holding hands, linking fingers
joining toes
making amends
waiting for the tide to turn
and the sky to start singing

as their love grows they lean
towards each other, their orbits touching
in the coldest of stellar reaches
their thought patterns merging
into a standing wave

it feels so good

a whisper spreads through
the gathering crowds lining the thoroughfares

those who pray and those who don't
of an impending miracle

formlessness to take form
the birth of a new star
the peeling away of a new cosmos

but nothing happens
that hasn't already happened,
the good moment slips by
like a blessing unseen
and the world doesn't hesitate
even for a moment
to go on its unblessed way

sister sun and brother moon
don't hold their breath
as they wait and love and love
and wait
side by side on a mossy wall
long forgotten

the night stealer

the night stealer sneaks in at night
and steals the world away
steals the sky, steals the stars
steals the moonlit bay

steals all the children too
who might come out to play

imagine, if you will,
an evil Father Christmas
Krampus himself
like a bad elf
who freaks around at the end of the day
stealing
presents from under the Christmas tree
even the sugar-plum fairy
in ballet tights
who stands at the very top of the tree
bearing the light

everything that once shone
becomes pale
and everything that once burst with colour

gets leached
and everything that once stood forth

disintegrates
and everything that was once full
becomes hollow
and everything that was found is lost

all the things that walk and crawl and wriggle
upon the earth
curl up their toes and shrink
back into themselves

they know what they're after
those night stealers
(they hunt in packs)
they go straight to the heart and soul of things
and proceed to feed
withering the grape on the vine
love in the heart
the song in the bell jar
the whisper of cosmic tides
disposing
what might have been precious
and turning it to dross

oh no, you can’t sleep easy
or sleep at all
when the night stealer comes
to steal the world away

in such unlikely circumstances love may be born

the Ferris wheel flies and Li'l Lucy lies
in a pink frenzy of candyfloss
butterscotch fingers
and eyes
too big for her stomach

the organ grinder grinds, the monkey cries
the comedy duo gathers in the laughs
while the melody lingers

Little Boy Lost hides
from the girl with the pink sugar lips
and satin ballet shoes
while the ghost train carries
all the Toy Town toddlers, every last one
into the glad mouth of their screams

Li'l Lucy wins a yellow bear
and wants to go home
she's nostalgic for a world that never was
for kisses that never were
but merely seemed

or the embrace of the bear, and an end
to all the happy lights that make her sad

while Little Boy Lost comes out of
the mirror with not a kill to his name
full of shame
with his jingling eyes
and his fencepost legs
happy to follow her
to the end of the dream

cowboy capers
(for David Gemmell)

sorcerous swords and six-guns -
the lone gunman sets out
across the vanishing plain

where a woman, her two children
and their covered wagon drawn by oxen
are winding their way to Paradise
which always comes with a clear stream
rich soils
healthy children and a good man

it's a big country

presently, a gateway to another world
will open between some standing stones
and demons will pour forth
demons that look like men, demons that
look like beasts, demons
that just look like demons
and they make short work of heroes

will the lone gunman be in time to save
the woman, and her children, and so earn
her eternal gratitude among

the piles of wasted ghouls
or will he be too late and find them
their bodies ripped and torn apart
by a hatred too vast for the human heart?

for her part, the woman's already had one man
die on her
she can't afford a second
wandering the Void in search of lost love
and, besides, grief lies like some special curse
on the Deathwalker, Demonslayer
not for one moment can he still
the crying of his heart

not the kind of man you settle down with

the lone gunman arrives at the mountains
the tracks are clear, they head west
into the sunset – knows a rare, quiet moment
with just himself and his grief under the stars

before all hell breaks loose

walking the shadow

Mr Moonlight walks his shadow
up and down the street
over the hills and far away

as he withdraws his will
from the sky and the earth
a new light arises

the ocean catches it
cradles it
turns it into a new day

a searing flame that lifts
from the horizon
to the cowl of night

where you'll find him
Mr Moonlight
walking his shadow

into the west

moments out of the box

these few moments must stand
for all those times we can't
and couldn't ever
spend together, all those things
we can't and couldn't ever do
the words we can't
and could never say

they are just ordinary moments
these few
nothing special and soon gone
but contain all that we were and could
have been
and never will

like the Petrushka doll you had
when you were nine
one moment unpacks another
and another, all moments contained
in the first
so brief it can't be measured
but must include
the scene on the balcony

under the sun
when something might have happened

or the moment on the bus, in the rain
when nothing did

these things lodge in the heart
to reappear on sunny days
or in the dark-dark wood
where there are only owl moments
with owl tears

then the heart might
skip a beat
or two
in remembrance

blossoms

dropping in
from here, there and everywhere
blossoms
from a fresher time

pink and red and rosey
cream along the edges
fresh from the tree, or someone's posy
they can slip through the air
as if on skis, turn corners
and gently flutter when love is near

like angel's tears, too soft to hold
they fall into the world as if it were a wedding
and they were the witnesses

they do not come from here
you know
but somewhere else, somewhere
that can't be named
for in the naming it would become
something other, but you know it
when you see it

that ethereality

that promise made to a broken land
the harbinger of good cheer

you know them, those blossoms
in all their other-worldliness
the only way you can know them
in the springtime of the world
here and there
and somewhere else
blossoms
from a fresher time

memories of an arrow

as the night fades
and the light is lush
nine suns appear
in the early world
competing for the sky

a multiple dawn
around a single horizon
nine eyes opening

a great fear comes
upon the earth
upon those who live
and those who scheme

when these nine suns
meet in the middle
of the air
what a falling out
there will be

our hero steps forward
with his mighty bow

and his golden arrows
and his gleaming hair

and his naked chest
glistening

sky and earth hang
in balance

the bow is drawn
the arrow fitted

the heart steady
the eye in line
muscles matched

those who live
and those who dream
hold their breath

and as the gods look
the other way
the first arrow flies

lullaby

I'll leave this space open for you
Mr Moonlight
I'll leave my door ajar
and when soft rain comes
to touch the world with bliss
I'll know it's you
and who you are

when nothing comes
but the open sky
clear of any scribbles
and there is no rain
in the world of light
I won't mind
too much
I won't hang out
because, you know
I've lots of places to be

but nowhere to go

I'll put a candle in the window
just in case

you can never tell

with Mr Moonlight
I'll leave the gate unlatched
with a note that reads like this

no strings attached
for just a single kiss

I'll leave this space for you
Mr Moonlight
open and asking
feasting and fasting
throwing wide the covers
smoothing the page
listening from afar

and when soft rain comes
to touch the world with bliss
I'll know it's you
and who you are

making it up

the constellations make a pretty sight
strung like Christmas lights on Mars
way up on high, curling
between
memory and makeshift and all the things
we read into the stars

they come down to earth from time to time
like gods are said to do
pretending to be toys, with eyes full of fire
arms full of gifts
and limbs full of spring

sing! they say, sing!

the constellations look just right
all dressed up for the party
strung across the sky
in one great scoop, making patterns
illusive to the eye

the patterns you find
are there because of the looking

projected from within
connecting of the dots on god's waistcoat

otherwise there's nothing there
but hurdy-gurdy
shapes
fashioned in the mind

all good things

it's hard to say goodbye
when the time comes around
to unplug
and put the words to bed

to quit the show
make other arrangements
say all those sorts of things
that have to be said

but always sound sort of empty
in the saying
like a wind-up toy praying

all good things must come to an end
so I've read

all that has been joined
will be broken

that pang in the heart is an echo
of many partings

stillness above, turbulence below

the toy box has come of age
even if the toys themselves have not
and the echo is of footsteps
heading off stage

for the toys themselves it's not
a farewell
but a change of location
to the pre-loved shop, perhaps
where some of the grander figures
like Big Ted and Barbie
might find a shelf at the right height
to sit and stare fixedly
off
into the far distance

I wouldn't read too much into it
if I were you
they are only toys, after all
only good for let's pretend
there's no heaven for them
or hell

no sun, no rain
no jam and toast
no cries, no laughter

they become the story
only if you make it up for them, keep
pretending,
keep offering them a fantasy life
in Toy Town
where they can walk a street
meet and greet
catch a train
and there are and never have been
any goodbyes

now the toy box is long gone
over the rise, under the rain
or filled with dusty old shoes

the valedections have been sung
or spoken

everyone else has grown up
and lived happily ever after

Book Two

Hide Your Eyes

The Rumi Poems

A rose's rarest essence
lives in the thorn

Rumi

Translation: Colman Barks, adapted.

No longer a stranger
you
listen all day
to these crazy love words

like a bee
you fill countless larders
with honey

though yours
is a long distance flight
from here

Rumi

Translation: Colman Barks, adapted.

WHERE THE TRUTH LIES

to cover the truth
with a handy lie
is to tell another kind of truth
about where truth lies

this is not as abstract as it sounds

lies hide
the most perfect truth of all
oh secret of my soul
oh Beloved of my heart
oh Guest of my flesh

make me whole
make me whole

lies show more than facts
which lack
that self-revealing fantasy touch
we bring to our lives
in the stories we tell each other
at bedtime
and in the morning

when we need to rise and shine
to pick up our narratives
where we left off
to get control where control
was lost

tears fly when this stuff
unfolds
when the lie and the truth lie down
together
and make up yet another good yarn
for the sake of the world
for the sake of our hearts

just to keep the narrative in line

give me a story we can recite
in all good faith
one we can chant
turn into ritual, an incantation
and bring us into our known world
with the least hassle

when the light goes out

RUMI'S LAMENT

Beloved!
there are times
when I am five miles high
enjoying the view
the clouds below
the void above
riding the bend of spacetime
waving my cowboy hat
and screaming whoopee

and other times
it's a fight to raise a smile
or find a rhyme
that doesn't show too clearly in the line

my name doesn't sound like me
anymore
I am not what I would be
I'm no dervish

I dance like a goose dreaming it's a swan
dive like a fish that's lost the sea

and fear the tears of the condemned
even as the drums roll
and the crowds whet their teeth
for the feast

I want more than a whore
I want it full bore
straight to the core
under the sheets of night

and a smorgasbord of stars
for our delight

let me see the Beloved smile

I want a theory of theories
that holds the big shout
with nothing left out
to wonder about
not just the mere cosmos
with its stupendous flights
dark planets and binary stars
but this stuff between my ears
hopes and tears
and all this thumpity-thump
of the heart

I'm no use if I can peer
behind the curtains of creation
and see the big bang in the making
hear the death rattle of the nation
yet can't track tears
from one side of my face
to the other

what's the use of being Rumi
if the left hand doesn't know
the right hand is its brother?

everybody's screaming
the deafening sound of lost love
but I'll sit with the quiet ones awhile
like you, Beloved
with your gentle face
and get a handle on it

if only
just for a moment
it would hold
in place

THAT GREATER FRENZY

it's a pretty mess
what to say and do
and how we make up for it all
when the word gets about
and the girls gather
to admire your dress

from the face in the sky
you can't hide your eyes
or keep your quiet
when sharp-toothed demons
run riot
and Rumi gets left
to wrtite on the wall
after the party
and everybody who's anybody
has gone home
with what's left of their lives

perhaps She could never stand
to have her bodice ripped
by eager slaves
that we might behold

all that is in bold and
open form
lest we die of awe
with no one to pour
a little wine on our graves

for surely
we would die from that greater frenzy
before getting the chance
to clear away the tears
close the accounts
say goodbye to friends and fears
make a final stand
prepare ourselves for obliteration
covering the eyes of our children
with our naked hands

UPSIDEDOWN

hanging from your ankles
it's a world upsidedown
although it's hard to see the upside
of it
from this angle

people walk around on their hands
trees wave their roots in the air
while flowers bloom underground
and the moon grows
at the bottom of a lake

Rumi has witnessed this many times
without having to be drunk
under the influence of the moon
in the embrace of the Beloved
or bound to a stake

that's not all, my furry friends
because upsidedown means back to front
and inside out
as north turns south
and east and west swap beds

a staircase that goes only one way
words that run away from themselves
even as they walk backwards
out of your mouth

and mothers that butcher babies
even as they suckle them
and men that own the world
even as they gut it
and leaves that drift upwards
in a hawk wind
and lovers that fall out of graveyards
freshly born

lies that grow wings
to become butterflies
and a wind that skids backwards
over the sand
lifting the world with it

and that's not all comrades
of the dark, supplicants forlorn,
there's so much more
where that came from

cause and effect get
turned around
with effects turning into causes
and causes turning into
effects

arguments get stood on their heads
blatant stupidity presented as policy
hatred as righteousness
bigotry as bravery
blindness as blessing
love as perversion
art as crime
dusk as dawn
theirs as mine

so don't expect too much
as you hang
downside of this upsidedown
side, trending upside soon, no doubt
when the truth comes out
when all will be
put the right way up
for the last time
so help us
for the last time

RUMI'S FIVE-FINGERED EXERCISES

don't set the bar too high
don't make the children cry
don't stone the crows that fly
don't make an honest man sly
don't raise that flag too high

don't make the children die
don't make your tears too shy
throw the bar into the sky
lift the children up on high
give the world a golden eye

RUMI'S TRIBUTE TO DR SEUSS

what you imagine you imagine
you imagine for real
everything else is a lie or a steal

everything else heads for the hills
everything else lives as it kills

don't be deceived by the girl at the pool
the shimmer and glimmer
as the lights grow dimmer
or the wise man in secret playing the fool
or the hypocrite in black copping a feel

what you imagine you imagine
you imagine for real

don't close your eyes when it's time to read
don't close your mouth when it's time to feed
don't shut your heart when it's time to bleed

what you imagine you imagine
you imagine for good
for bad or for worse or for love
of a deal

everything else is a maybe, perhaps
or a would
just something you heard
some gossipy rumours, a twisted word
randomly said
improperly read

what you imagine you imagine
changes the world
turns the stars around
turns love on its head
a tree into a high-flying bird

don't look the other way
when you're ready to play
what you imagine you imagine
won't go away

SEE-SAW

did you see what you thought
you saw
or was the see-saw purely
for the playground
where children scream
and throw their hands into the air
and the Beloved walks the street unseen
and unrecognised
secret lover of her heart disguised

I saw what I thought I saw
because I couldn't see anything else
ever
what I thought I saw is all I see
for all eternity
and the poet was just so right
when he said that one thought
can fill immensity

what I thought I saw, I saw
and can't unsee
no matter how hard I try
or what's at stake

or how the heart
might hide the world
from the naked sky
or the naked sky might
hide the heart
from the world

it works whichever way you say it

all in hiding
from that invisible worm
that flies the night
and heedlessly buries itself
in the heart of the rose

PAN LOVE

when Pan comes to town
he sleeps where he will
and enters dreams and bodies
and dream bodies
and body dreams
without so much as a please
or thank you

happy to be man or woman
as desire pleases
to shapeshift into the image
of the Beloved
(what's your pleasure?)
and to blow into the reeds
a melody so poignant
the heart melts
and the body opens
and the blood rises
and the rose turns
as Pan enters
and all the nymphs rejoice
to hear
the cries that go up to heaven
the ecstatic prayers

ascending to heaven
the prayers and pleas of helpless
throats
seeking the very tongue of heaven

leaving only the men and women
with their ordinary lives
on an ordinary morning
in the wreckage of their gardens
and their god-struck eyes

holding the baby

CATS AND MONKEYS

monkey swings along
the monkey bars
chittering and chattering
making up stories
never missing a beat
quicker than a flash
spreading the heat
opening the word
emptying the word
making love to the fair
flesh on fire, making love
to the very lineaments
of desire

no monkey this
no monkey moment either
swinging beyond
the teeth and the hair
wood and ash
the innocent and the liar

meanwhile
the yellow-eyed cat

parts the shadows
slips between the shadows
of the heat
bides its time
divides its time
purrs its time

nature breathes
the sweetest perfumes

and monkey never misses a beat

BETWEEN THE SHEETS

and you face the terror of knowing
that there is no in-between
knowing
and not knowing
between
love and death
between
the left and the right side
of the pumping heart

between seeing and seeing
and not being

there's
no scalpel sharp enough
to divide
love from love
nor wisdom enough
to bring them together
convincingly
for some sweet pillow talk

and as for your hands, well
they know where they've been
and you know it's best
when the left hand knows
what the right hand is doing
and they do it together
in mutual consent

there is no Goldilocks
moment
between high moon and
low sun
between melody and memory
between the penny and the penny arcade
between the moment of light
and the eternity of dark
between the devil
and the deep blue sea

between is a hard place to find
except between the sheets
somewhere between staying and fleeing

my god! the stars should be so wide
your heart a vessel of infinite depth
for your blood to race through

arteries of the earth and all her sister worlds
with you, you
mistress of all you behold
empress of all that ever was and will be
a tongue that arcs between the light
and the light

meanwhile, up dawn creeps
while your back is turned
shadows steal shadows out of the night
and you face the terror of knowing
there is no in-between
and no way of being
a goddess with a divided heart

except between the sheets

SACRIFICE

it was the touch that did it
the sacred touch
the touch that lights up
everything it touches

lightning-rod of the body
flesh of flesh, spark of spark
and the in-between of the flesh
where flesh parts
and love leaves its mark

feet that walk you over the earth
down the hall
through the archway and into the temple
hands held before you
beyond the last full stop
through the sweating graves
and beyond
far from the dreams and fears of men
through a land without remorse
your feet will keep you walking

where you have strayed
there is no quarter asked for
no prisoner taken
no last-gasp cigarette
not the echo of a prayer
your feet will keep you walking
from the hall to the temple to the isle
to the sanctuary
where a bed of soft flowers
has been prepared
fragrances shared
in the intimate bower

the sword cuts where it
will cut
the flowerhead lies
face up
your lover lies face down
your abnegation knows no bounds

your intestines are held in place
by faith alone
your legs walking you
by faith alone
as you draw near
a ladderless climb

through even the loneliest
of places
the barest of hills, slave-driven cities
mad kings
and wars against babies

you will hardly care
for already you can smell it
the heady incense in the air
the fragrance of her hair

as you light the candle
you'll know
this one flame can tear worlds
obliterate pasts
turn fancy into shame
make a mess out of blame
and dumb lies
and all the bobs and whistles
of a good life well lived

in the end it's the journey itself
that holds you, blindsided
hearing the siren cry
over the horizon
on the other side of the ocean

on the other side of the storm
but close
right in your ear
breathing in your ear
breathing from real lips
hearing the tingling breath
hearing the fall, the tumbling fall
the crying avalanche
of waves on rocks
all that the wisperings entice
and more, for the heart of the ocean
lies with the shore

as you reach for the knife
your hands have lost their tremble
your legs have given up walking
and you are at last
ripe
and ready for the sacrifice

INTOXICATION

make your peace, find your grace
peel your skies back

make moon eyes at the Beloved
embrace the warm ground

slip through the mirror
into a sweet elfin dream

hold hands with your delightful double
travel to impossible galaxies

paint the town red
hum with your own body electric

linger in scented gardens
drink from an overflowing cup

sleep the sleep of sweetness
in the sweetness of sleep

all of these things and more
lie within your compass
and suggest themselves
to the waking mind
the ever-tricksy mind
and the honest heart
most honest heart
never to part

but come home at night
to a light on the porch
some salad, still fresh
a piece of Christmas cake
(no longer fresh)

and a little something left in the bottle

SOMETHING FOR THE FERRYMAN

pennies fell from heaven
then they didn't

someone else must've needed them

we collected what we could
while we could
those we were able to find
in likely and unlikely places
scurrying about
here, there and everywhere
like blind ants at a picnic

pennies from heaven
heaven's graces

wow! we thought
the lord of all
must have deep pockets
deeper than our hopes
deeper than the world
deeper than love

and we are such greedy little creatures
we always want a little extra
please

oh, we hardly dared
count our blessings
even as we spent them
there were pennies everywhere
falling night and day
out of the generous sky
so who would worry
tomorrow as always
has to take care of itself
and all the other tomorrows
crowding in
are on their own

today is a big enough handful
even with pennies galore
somebody wants more
somebody has less
and we need a few for the cake

it's every man for himself
by the look of things

we took them for granted, I suppose
those passing pennies
we always had our hands in our pockets
a rosy fire in our bellies
and something for the ferryman

then they stopped
the sky was full then it was empty
there were no more pennies
not even for the cake

I guess they were never ours
in the first place
they were passing by
and while one side might have borne
the image of plentitude and
sheaves of corn
the other
was none other
than the face of hunger

THE QUICKENING

something always quickens
in the deep
that's what the deep is for

could be love, could be war

with the quickening
comes the awakening
and with the awakening
comes the hunger
and with the hunger
comes the clawing and pawing
the drilling and killing
promise and betrayal

I'm not sure what to do with this
which way to turn
which doors to open and
which to close
and who might already have
come and gone

follow the quickening
consecrate the awakening
feed the hunger

and doors will open and close
by themselves
as if under ghostly influence
landscapes
and possibilities of landscapes
will rush by
like a cascade of prophesies
and all things possible
will be possible

and when that glad day comes
there will once more be the deep
the deep stillness of the deep
where something quickens

it always does

TWO BREATHS HAVE I

you have a breath
a dark breath
you have a breath
a light breath

each one to the other
is a reflection
of that which might be
if everything else were
in balance

if everything else were even-stevens
all being equal, one breath
would usher the next
with an easy reciprocity

one's out to the other's in
one's in to the other's out
mist on the mirror

it all comes out in the wash
they say
but I don't know about that
anymore

what should come quite naturally
turns out to be
an exercise in metaphysics
with the dark breath and the light
breath
taking place
way beyond the body
somewhere
with the mirror turned
to face the other way
to the other side of the self
where breath becomes light

you have a body
a dark body
you have a body
a light body

each in love with the other
the other in love with each

MOST GENTLE REVENGE

good friends and comrades
be gentle
with those who hurt you
for they hurt worse

their wound
is double yours

and besides
it's always ten times worse
to be forgiven
than to be accused
so you have the satisfaction
of knowing
that your gentle solicitation
cuts
far deeper
than any knife

SHE'S NOT WHAT SHE SEEMS

cultivate the Beloved
at great risk to life and limb
she's not what she seems

however nice it might feel
her lips on yours
her hand on your thigh
the softest part
there's a joker in the deal
a scratch that won't heal
a heart that won't feel
a hand that can't cry

once there was order
order sweet order
sequence and sequins
procession possession succession

then the Beloved comes through the door
everything flies up and about
a big whirly shout
and the ceiling becomes the floor

there's a poltergeist loose
look out
watch for fallout
for the drunken goose
for the lame excuse

and that broken cup
the one your grandmother gave you
from another age
the famous one
can't be glued back together
without the seams showing
to the careful eye

it's just not the same, is it?
best bury it with honours
and real tears
and put your signature
to the memory
before signing off
cultivate the Beloved and you might die
since in death life grows new wings
sprung from painfully human shoulders

and it's hard to know
what you are
let alone what you are becoming

CULTIVATION

allow time for it
give it space, room to grow
to show its face
to come clean, to make amends
put on a show
declare its intentions
colour its petals pink

things do not come forward
of their own accord
but need a little coaxing
a little stroking under the chin
a few sweet nothings
for the shy one, the shyest of all
the veiled one
the whispered one
who parts her flesh
only to the red dawn and no other

until tomorrow
this gift of flowers

try
a little humming at the back of the throat
a light drumming of fingers on stretched skin
a thrumming on the kettledrum
an up-tempo two-step
a platter of memories and a book of hours

allow time for it
to arrive, to be

give it a place and
space
a touch of grace
and there it is

quivering and uncertain
but alive
oh yes, alive

NEXT TIME AROUND

this time around
you came to it late
so late
leaning to one side
like the walking wounded
like the last bird in the nest
with too much past, not enough future
and a muddled vision

there was a lot going on you didn't know about
you turned your face the other way
hid your eyes
and never once had to think
about the *this* and the *that*
and worlds unseen
the peripheral stink
the paraphernalia of a collision
with the Beloved

coming to, you didn't know
the place
for what it was
or yourself

for what you had once been

after all that forgetting
you couldn't find your bearings
and the compass swung wildly about
in search of directions

your feet didn't know their left
from their right
let alone your mouth find
the right inflections

the rain felt unfamiliar
on your face
and the furnace in your lungs
appeared to come, by the taste of it,
from another planet
where there are creatures who talk
with their skin
paint with scent
and make love with their voices

it took a long time to understand
the *whys*, the *whiches* and *wherefores*
let alone the *neverthelesses*
and the *notwithstandings*

you weren't accustomed
to this sort of treatment
the summary executions
and the bright-edged laughter
the boot through the brain at 3 a.m
the shakes at breakfast

you weren't accustomed to people
who smile on the other side
of their faces
and whose words grow backwards
into their mouths
like eager parasites

where the sun is turned inside out
and men go to work inside their briefcases
and somebody has to pay for everything
except what's owed

you didn't have the stomach
for that sort of thing
and who could blame you
for dragging the chain
and looking about for another
chance

you couldn't hold onto a childhood
that was only in your mind
as if there were some comfort there
some refuge
some sweet ease for the heart
knowing how foolish that is
but being foolish anyway
because folly was all that was left
in the heat of the moment

it's different now
you've caught up
not running behind on little legs
crying 'wait for me!'
you have come home
and seen the place as it always was
but could never be
seen worlds come together and part
seen the fantastic lie down
with the ordinary

little wonder you came to it late
but, you know, late is just in time

this time around

THE WAITING GATE

it had to turn out the way it did
there was no other way
no other shape to make

not because of some destiny
or extraordinary fate
or having to play god's catspaw
but the confluence of events
and energies, hopes and fears
memories
and all the trappings of the self

approach the gate
open the gate
take the gate in your mouth

there are choices galore
but only one you can take
and there comes a time
in the space of a breath
when all roads lead back
to the same place
the same beach

the same stand of trees
the same squally sky
up the garden path
around the pond and
through the gate
the waiting gate
the hidden door
to the other side where there are
no gates, nor fences
nor enclosed spaces, nor
rusty books of law

just the taste of the susceptible air
the unbarred sunlight
and maybe somebody
walking beside you holding your hand
by the fingertips
but you can’t see them
feeling as alone as alone could be
crying like a child cries
who can’t be seen or heard

the Beloved standing at the threshold
like an orphan

and when you try to close the gate
there is no gate
to close
just a graffiti-covered wall

and you knew, then and there
that it would have to turn out
the way it did

THE BELOVED RULES

I went to the Beloved
full of excuses
and met you there

it was an awkward moment
excuses all around

I had to laugh
the look on your face
your voodoo walk
the sudden terror of the blood

a great unexpectedness
opened up like a water lily
with you the dragonfly
wings iridescent
hovering over the still water

we exchanged politenesses
as many as were needed
then kissed like crazy
because that was the only thing
left to do

you can't script these things
you can't imagine them
you can't believe them
but in the land of the Beloved
the Beloved rules
her face everywhere
on every billboard and bleacher
screen and scene

we knew why we were there
and who was to blame
and where judgement might fall
but what the hell
by the time the kissing was done
and we were getting naked
we ran right out of excuses
though we had plenty to spare

and rose from the dead
feeling the wind in our hair
the blood in our veins
the bubble of words on our lips

and the hand we were
each to each
holding

THE GIFT

on the street mourners gather
the shadow of the mountain
stretches across the plain

a woman waits by a crayon-blue tree
wind picking at her skirt
trying to remember the sky

from her secret hide out
a little girl watches
birds turning into fish
and trees with their hearts on fire
and a sky that unwinds
into the night

a great astonishment of being
you could never have guessed

the girl returns
under a sky of juicy stars
through the shaows of many worlds
to the secret lover of her soul
the crayon woman

who
coils into bed with her
caresses her memories
and whispers into her ear
incantations that bare the body
and saturate the spirit

mourners return to the mountains
the woman returns to the sky
the girl rises into new day

THE DESERTER

I couldn't stand watch for you
during the night
my faith firm, texts memorised
because the night was endless
an endless night
(we couldn't end this night)
the air too cold
and the morning too long ago
to be properly recalled
or accounted for
in this neverending war

I didn't have the heart for it
and started to see things
to smell people long dead
fucking in their graves
their bones crunching together
to hear gargoyles rutting in the shadow
of the eaves of overgrown temples
with the temple whore
and forgot to sing

you stole all the heat
on your quest for the perfect love
the most rapturous, most transcendent
love
to the shivering core
a healing touch
to the soul's own sore

more heat than the body can take
spilling out into the night
the colder-than-hell night
the bogeyman night

I was to stand watch
with prayers at the ready
over this most fragile thing
the spirit of a newborn
about to be wed
to be, and to be more
but at the first hapless cry
and indrawn breath
I turned tail and fled

THE TRANSFORMATION

Rumi knows the secret
of the soul's furtive lover
who approaches unbidden
partially hidden
bearing the midnight flame
and a woodland touch

Rumi calls her the Guest
and guest she is
more than a ghost
a midnight flush in red
or a visitation from his head
the Guest walks through the poet's heart
through the heavenly host
and the kingdom of the beast
to sit down at the feast without a blush
calls for wine and dancing
makes a huge fuss
while the gossips all gossip
from behind their hands
and nothing gets said

poets prepare the way
strewing flowers on the bed
and words every which way

with an expectant heart
and labouring breast
hands do a little ballet
on the pillow
where her head will rest

she might come, or she might not
she is like the wind that way
hither and thither
like a dandelion seed

hear her cries
wherever the wind holds sway
glimpsed only
when deep in play
whose laughter fades to gray
when the sun will rise

nothing more than a whisper
on the curtain
as the curtain parts
and the window reveals

the garden and moon-child
in full voice
as the song starts

she is
hidden but not hidden
hidden in plain sight
plain as night
standing before you
the soul's clandestine lover
image of the Beloved

RESPECTING THE GUEST

when the Guest arrives at the door
make her welcome
give her a hug and offer her
some kitchen clatter
a drink or a little more

the blessings of the house
and some light chatter
if you must

it may be best, my profligate lover,
to think of her
as a messenger from beyond the mind
a manifestation of earth and sky
and all that lies between
seen and unseen
a pagan spirit of a kind
complete with twigs and leaves
and pixie dust

a song from a far star
that fell with a shock

think of her as a tree, a rock,
a quiet stream
rain after a drought
a clear sky above the flood
rising above flesh and blood
and everyday lust

she is upswept and in step
cool and sweet
as fragile as a love lyric
as strong as a prayer
the gold clasp in her hair

she is the Guest

not a manifestation
of the lunar day
or convocation of numbers
or the fevers of Rumi
with his hectic lines
and his heart
breaking apart

but rather
clothed in human flesh
held together

by trembling bones
with a dry mouth
and a thudding pulse

no messenger at all, actually
but from the self
to the self
witnessed in the words
of the poet
who only seeks to give her
the best the house can offer

THE NATURE OF THE GUEST

the Guest comes
only when she is called
when your pleas
resonate with her blood

I have no mouth but I must scream
reads a title from the shelf
among your books of wisdom

that's why the Guest is here
why you find her at the table
or under the rose bush
in the scent of manuka blossom
the twittering of a skylark
or the austere warmth of a lily

in the end there is no escaping her
she has come to give your face its mouth back
to open the voice in your chest
to watch you part your lips

and hear you scream

WARM THE TEA ON A GENTLE FLAME

it's okay to dread
the arrival of the Guest
the twitch of the curtain
the slip and the flirt

you can't know
exactly what she brings
but that it will shake you
it will break you
even as she sits and sips her tea
adjusts her skirt
and lights up with glee

best make no plans

afterwards
after all that came before
she will take out her lyre
tease its strands
and sing you a refrain
not even Rumi could devise
for it admits no boundaries
but its own dripping notes

of rain and fire
and the secret melodies
of her hands

a song like that
can change you, exchange you
and when you turn to look back
everything you can see
the whole affair
has disappeared, like a gate
that was never there

it's okay to dread
the arrival of the Guest
for there's no predicting
the twist of the lyric
the turn of your heart
or where the galaxy is bound

but there's no getting around it
the Guest will arrive
the Beloved will do the same

you might as well prepare
the saucer and the cup
and warm the tea on a gentle flame

THE GARDENIA

in the inner chambers
with the sound of water slipping
over mossy stones
you remove her veil

it's made of starlight and lace
edged in snowflake
and myth
with a touch of yellow
at the centre
for secret love

this is the moment
this is what you came here for
what has had you on edge
all these years
from the time you first
took the sky into your chest

like a swan you glide over
your disturbing shadow

hiding your eyes away
from petals of deft light
and the sly laughter of girls

whenever you walked into the wild
she was there, a power
so elemental
you didn't know her for what she was
or hear any wedding sounds

when the wild comes into you
a storm on the sky's wing
or in the stillness of green
to rattle your heart
she walks alongside
she opens your past
to show you
its invisible hiding places

how could you not
lead her into the garden
saturated by the scent of gardenias
blinded by their purity
inhale her scent
where the sunlight falls
and the world is quicksilver and dapple

lift her veil of starlight and lace
and see what there is
to be seen

a corolla of elegant white

THEY'RE HERE

tyres crunch on the gravel
the wine teeters
on the rim of the glass
music softly plays
a door opens and closes

in shuttered rooms men decide
the fate of the world
who will live and who will die

indistinct laughter is heard
from the bushes, the rhododendrons
and the chrysanthemums
in the warming air
where the children run and have their fun
wherever the devil may dare

girls and boys come to play
the moon doth shine as bright as day

and out they come, like forest sprites
like a trick of the light
holding hands and cartwheeling

to the effervescent action
of their limbs
free of care
creatures of earth and air

footfalls thud in the hallway
the wind trembles in the glass
music swells
and the voices rise in sweet descant
as the earth tips in its sleep
and all things come to pass

come with a whoop and come with a call come with
good will or not at all

you can hear the children
they come up out of memory
break the surface with a song
and you are ready
ready-steady
as the beast approaches
and the wine spills

as ready as you'll ever be
to join them

up the ladder and down the wall a halfpenny roll
will serve us all

THE WOODEN SPOON

Rumi lays out his breakfast
roasted oats, warmed goat's milk
and a dish of honey

he says a quick prayer or two
in case god snatches it all away
before he can lift a spoon

there have been times when
the spoon has left the bowl full
but landed empty on his lips

god can be that quick

once a thief stole the moon from his sky
leaving his window empty for many nights
and a sack of sorrow in his gut

it took a heap of prayers and invocations
to get it back
but the thief had consumed all
but a thin slice
which

with more prayers
and invocations
grew once more into full size
in Rumi's window
large and tasty looking

as he eats, he savours every mouthful
chew for long enough and it all tastes
like god
or tomorrow's grief or joy

he needs all his strength
his humility
he needs his bloodsong
all the magic he can muster
incantations and chants
and age-old prayers

it is said that when he was young
he made birds out of clay
and threw them in the air
where
they turned into real birds
and flew away

but none of that is true
all made up for popular consumption
and to keep his ratings high

the only magic the poet has
lies in his ordinariness
his scuffed slippers, frayed cuffs
his wooden spoon
and the wild beating
of his dervish heart
as he sets out into the day

to meet the Beloved

ALL THAT'S LEFT

Rumi can barely make it
from the door to the gate
and back again

he can't shake fate
he can't create
his hands won't mend

his skin reeks of the grave
ashes cover his head
tears drip into his wine
ants cover his sheets
dead birds flitter his skies
his lines are inconsolable

his words are gone
all the gold and silver ones
set in their sparkling syntax
glitter
and wink out

all that's left is lies

Beloved, let's fill his cup
lift him from the dead
raise him up
reflesh his bones

let the breath in his chest
move sure and steady
one and another to follow

set him walking

the Guest is coming tomorrow
and Rumi is not ready

THE STENCH

Rumi found something putrid
at the bottom of his garden
something that stank

among the slugs and snails
and maggoty, rotting things
he found something more rank
than nature could devise

a sham
seasoned with deception
wrapped in a lie
that won't break
down
into smaller
bits
because, at the heart of it,
pretense is indivisible
and timeless

Rumi lost his voice
the two sides of his throat

were stuck together
words turned turd

as he bent to take a
closer look
a shadow fell
blotting out the sky
the world turned dark
before his eyes

the wheat, the corn
the leafy greens
and the tiny forget-me-nots
that border the herb patch
and all the slugs and snails
and creeping things
and a sky that flies them all

blotted out
until nothing that was light
was left
except the putrid thing
the false thing
which glowed
like a lump of radioactive
protoplasm

which Rumi tried to bury
with his bare hands and his bare words
in the empty dark

MEETING RUMI AT THE CROSSROADS

at the crossroads
many tracks
led off
to many worlds
true and fake
and multiplying pathways
I could take

to cultivate friends
avoid enemies
and get in good with god

I found a venerable ancient
dressed in Sufi robes
with eyes that veered apart
one to the light, one to the dark

in some other world his double
was busy dancing
to the whirl of his robes
and the thunder of drums

I wasn't going to stop
he's the sort of person you'd
sneak past
in case he reads you a fortune cookie
the worst of fates
but I wasn't to be let off that fast

you want to know which road to take
he said
no, I said, I had my pride
everywhere I went it was by my side

he shook his head
'there are no crossroads,' he said

was this my fortune cookie
my inescapable fate?

'there are no decisions to make
there is only one road to take
all you have to do is walk it'

I waited for the crossroads to vanish
and my road to show itself
that I may walk it
and in that time of waiting

the venerable ancient
wrote many poems, lifetimes of lines
in many worlds, and many histories
and became famous and much studied
by all the universities
in the multiverse
and finally died with honour
or an unmarked grave

the crossroads didn't magically vanish
but I didn't want
to hang around the spooky old wizard
with his veering eyes

the only road
was the one I was walking
so I kept putting one foot
in front of the other
always my best foot forward
sure and steady

'You see', the poet said,
'it is the road that walks

A CREATURE WHO WALKS UNSEEN AMONG US

on the road
I died
and had to come back to life
again
all by myself
to walk amongst you

I had to reassemble
my wits
out of all the floating bits
and the flying bits
and the dying bits
and the rumbling, grinding bits
and the bits that didn't fit
the other bits

it was hard work
constructing myself
into a form recognisable
that would pass among the people
as the up and walking
up and talking

real thing
I didn’t see a tunnel, or light
to guide my path
or friends waiting to usher me
into the great unknown
rather the steady chant of the poet
reciting the sacred syllables
the many names of god
echoing through the dimensions
that lie
between the land of the living
and the land of the hopeful

I could sing along
after a fashion
as the words were new
fresh as spring
bright as a cornfield
hot as a passion

now I walk
under different stars
made
for an unfamiliar sky
in quite another place
but no matter

what really counts is
that I am alive
after having died

and maybe not for the first time

STAYING AWAKE

Rumi is tired
from all this quivering
and shivering
quaking and shaking
spasms of fire
and wants to lie down
and sleep
the sleep of the newly born

even a wooden pillow
and iron blankets
feel soft
in the body of sleep
a satiny oblivion
in the deep place beyond space
beyond even the shadow
of desire

but he is fast learning
the price he has to pay
for fleshing himself in the world
as he did, quite recklessly
for being a human being

in the human-created world
and suffering all the ills
the flesh is heir to
even as the world is stolen away

he lights up like a filament
electrified from head to toe
too weary to dance and half in trance
he's made sick
with love

it seems he has understood
too late
what happens after all this courting
and hectic pursuit of the Beloved
who after all
may not wish to be seen
and may try to hide inside a face
only to be discovered
in the deepest recesses of
wakefulness

TRY SOMETHING NEW

if you feel your heart
is about to burst out of your chest
in a spray of blood and foam
and palpitating muscle

maybe it will
maybe that time has come
maybe it's the right thing

if you feel you'll die on the spot
from the touch of love
and the trees and the tangle
of the moon in the trees
and waves of sourceless pleasure

maybe you will
maybe that time has come
maybe it's the right thing

if you feel as if your lungs
are about to cave in
to let in the cold, airless void

between huddles of stars
where there's nothing but god to breathe

maybe they will
maybe that time has come
maybe it's the right thing

if you feel that your legs
are about to give out
and you'll fall over on the street
or while taking a pee
maybe they will
maybe they already have
maybe you're already crawling
towards that ever more distant
horizon
that's rushing towards you
away from you
and you can only propel yourself
forward
on your elbows
when even your knees have given out

or pull yourself along
by the willpower of your fingers alone

until there's nothing left
to get a hold upon

then maybe all that
has already happened
heart lungs and muddy blood
and all the things death feels like

so on the count of three
as in one-two-three
I want you to feel something

altogether quite different

CALL UP THE SPIRITS

wind slamming
lightning makes a play
swelling oceans
of blood and guts
stars like skin piercings
nights like death

and the news, the news, the news
is never good

the moon
the Guest, the Beloved
always disappearing
only to creep back up
among the feathery grasses
and mottled shades of the garden

the silky scent of red clover
heady oreganum steeped in the past
thyme that whistles at love

all dressed up with nowhere to go

the ancestors come crowding around
with their desperate histories
their hands breaking open
their eyes in chains
crying out for justice
for flesh, for pleasure
for redress
for well-earned oblivion

you have a children's rhyme
stuck in your throat, a chant
half born
a name that doesn't stick
an angel with folded wings
a passion too big for its boots
you are ready to run
ready to cry

and you can't shut your ears
to the mocking sound of children
the shame and disgrace
and choked up tears

sticks and stones
will break your bones
but names
will never hurt you

SENSUAL SENSES

that smell of cinnamon spice
like the smell of wool burning
rich and oily

the chirp of the nightingale
is like a distant call
from a morning that comes too early

the smell of the earth
and the moist decay of the ponga fronds
is like the damp on your thighs

the touch of the cardamon night
on your bare skin
has its own intimacy

the way the flowers taste your tongue
is enough to set the garden alight
with a late sunset

and the sight of all you can't see
comes as a revelation
just on time

FEEDING TIME

the hunter hunts
the prey has choices
one is to the other
matched
so they tell us

the killing and the willing
but there are shades
of blood and heat
of willing meat
and shades of honest doubt
against the black and the white
and the red
amid the spunk and gore
to come

the hunter may talk to his prey
quite soothingly
and strike when the time is right

the prey may run or demure
or fight, or unveil their hearts
or limp, or play victim

the sweet surrender
the most playful sacrifice
the enticement and rejection
the heartbreak and final squeal
of resignation
as the hunter strikes

and something gets to feed
in the feeding night

MAKE A RUN FOR IT, FRIEND

when the Beloved comes along
better hide your face
or make a run for it
scatter to the four winds
while there's still time
and a rhyme or two remains

she takes no prisoners
and can slay you with her eyes alone
a mere glance
right and left, men and women
and all those in between
fall over backwards, unbelieving

when she walks the street
fixtures become unfixed
lampposts float sideways
on their pools of sodium light
parking meters joust
shop mannequins seduce customers
with porcelain words
money bursts into flame in pockets
and cash registers

the coffee sits on top of the cream
and there's blood on the ground
from all the hearts that have jumped
right out of their time
and eyes everywhere you look
from those who have torn them out
to hang on trees like rotting fruit
until the trees go blind

it can get that bad, dear friend

terror
and evil visions to the gatekeepers
and the midnight horrors to
the devisers of laws and regulations
the *delirium tremens* to the sober
infinities to the mathematicians
and abstractions to the physicist

everywhere she goes
she'll piss on the pompous
puke on the puritan, mangle marriages
blur boundaries
tap on windows, rap on doors
hide up the street
vanish into forests of flame

lie beside you at night

with her breath upon you
and before you know it
put her hand right through your flesh
to put a little squeeze on your heart
just to remind you

and you, fool,
who forgot to run and failed to hide
have hardly known
a more
blissful ride

CUTTING UP SHADOWS INTO SYLLABLES

Rumi stays at home
making syllables out of the darkness
and, like blowing kisses,
sends them off into the night
into the care of the vagrant winds

he keeps thinking he has
better things to do
but can't think of what
at that moment

everybody is out having fun
dancing and whooping it up
embracing the moonlight
before dawn catches them out

but the lovesick Rumi
is not among them

rather
summoned from the forests of night
to mutter under his breath

frown at the shadows
and wonder how the moon
could get off scot-free
he remains home in chains
amid the wreckage left behind
by a visit from the Beloved

now look at him, scribbling words
like little paper birds
cutting up shadows into syllables
and, like blowing kisses,
sending them off into the imperfect night

STAR JUMPER

Rumi dreamed he became a frog
leaping from star to star
without raising a sweat

and breaking the shimmering surface
of spacetime
with his bulbous eyes wide

he isn't the only one
the whole cosmos is filled
with hopping frogs

frogs that hop in
from other universes
even unhopping frogs
that leap backwards
in time

he wakes full of regrets
for being a man
with toenails and underpants
all that baggage
and a dusty walk home

he can't even call himself a tadpole
with a shred of self-respect

no cosmos leaping for him
he can barely hop from the bed
to the door and from the door
to the gate

it's all one foot in front of the other
while one gets left behind
to drag up the rear

a far cry from star-leaping frogs
and a menagerie of other transformations
of which the poet can only dream

stones that turn into birds
as they skip across the inverted pond
of the sky
and the chitter of the skylark
turning into the music of the spheres
and the invention of galaxies
that turn constellations into
ripe fruit

all of these things
and the cartwheeling music

are one and the same as Rumi himself
if he only could see

he is the frog
his mind is the lily pad
and all he has to do is leap about

little wonder being a man
hardly cuts the mustard
nice as it is to have warm blood
and quickening affections

his life is like a turntable turning
in one direction
playing one song only
following as predictably
as lunch follows breakfast

and he finds himself sinking
sinking into the mire
into the mirror
for he has forgotten how to leap
how to break the shimmering surface
breathe
and to set his sights
on the next star

THE GRAND MASTER OF REGRETS

I have no regrets, I said to Rumi
but he didn't believe it
he's heard it all before
and said the same thing himself
on many occasions

it's the sort of thing people say
when things aren't looking too good

to regret is to be human, he said
but it sounded far too pompous
as if he were trying to be Confucius
instead of the poet with twigs
in his hair
large froggy feet
a few leftover phrases
from the dance of the god-driven

and so many goddamn regrets
he's lost count

along with faces and names
and missed opportunities

and stolen eternities
and days lost to the silly business
of having to be human
and keep up appearances
wearing clothes, eating all the time
nodding and smiling, pissing, preening
and pretending

you could say that Rumi
is the grand master of regrets
which is why
I've gotta have them too
you see
because he couldn't be alone
in something like that
suffering is isotropic
and the broken-hearted
never believe in love

I'm not so sure
I leave my regrets at the door
and forget to collect them
when I leave

a little trick I picked up
from Rumi in his better days

when he knew how to leave stuff behind
and never had to cross the same river
twice

but the poor poet has forgotten
how to laugh
and can't bear the thought of it

I try to get him on a jolly trolly, but you
know how it is with the broken-hearted
all he wants to do is drink
and talk to the moon

most of us have better things to do

TIME KILLS

you have to pause a while
to feel the full weight of this

you have to give it
due consideration

the sun that rose brightly
sinks into a murky haze

the heart that started out so eager
begins to labour

and (take a deep breath)

a thought you could once live with
becomes unsupportable

they say you have a receptive heart
but you know the moment
when it turned to iron
and what was okay
sort of
was not okay anymore

ever

you have to pause a while
for the reality of it all
to sink in
and oh how far it sinks!

now you can join Rumi
in his happy hell
and let him know the bad news

NO GETTING OFF THE HOOK

the scary part is
that there is no fate
to fate us
or destiny
to destiny us
or even god to god us

or fix us in some stupid future
among a host of futures

there's just us and us
and all that we pretend

the scary part is
that we are required to act
to move our mouths
and not have some other agency
move them for us

to pick up this and let go that
in good time and without losing
balance

to make something different
a little less stupid
and a little more to the point
we might just out-fate fate
leave destiny in the dust
and god on the hook
while we get on with it

THE EMPTY BOAT

Rumi knows what it's like
to slip like an empty boat
over still water
and be a host to grief
while bravely working

he knows what it's like
to empty the house
for the arrival of the Guest
and make paper chains
for the festivities
even as he plans his exit

he knows how it feels
to bite back tears
and fears
when contemplating the horrendous
state of the world
in its holocaust of madness

he knows that lovers are sleepless
because they feel the secret solitude
of the Beloved all around them

Rumi knows what it's like
to have his words fall flat
just like that
no taking them back
Jack
they're already done
rare, medium, burnt to a crisp

he knows what it's like
to be a cow that flies
or a goat that barks
or a chicken that never
comes home to roost

all of these things he knows
and other things
too wild to relate
because we'd have to draw
oceans above the sky
and make decent intervals
indecent
until we hardly knew our stops
from our starts

better to leave him in his empty boat
in his boatlessness in his tearlessness

in his wordlessness
in his indecency and his
secret solitude

and be on our way

IF JUST FOR ONCE

the urge to do something new
got Rumi off his backside
putting on a new coat
and opening some new doors
walking some new streets
breathing some fresh air
spitting out some old words
and generally seeing the world
in a novel way

he'd had enough of the same old
same old it was time to blow things wide apart
with a kiss
or something a little stronger

it was time to vanish into an ant's head
in front of a vast crowd
of screaming fans
or turn into a brightly plumed
bird of wonder
at a poetry convention
and fly off into the sun
in lyrical grandeur

a final gesture to time and circumstance

in short, here was an opportunity
amid the wreckage
to quit fooling around with heartbreak
and mooning over the Beloved
to pull up his socks
tie his shoelaces in a neat bow
and turn a corner before it disappears

everything and anything is possible
he wouldn't want his face to fix
in any particular grimace
in case the wind changed
and the grimace stayed forever

he wouldn't want to stick with
some style of walking
like a prisoner in chains
or find himself laughing at stale jokes
in a stale house
where it's either too early or too late
or any other unthinkable fate

let his face be an open book
let his love-struck eyes tell all

to all who tell
let his hands open and shut like sea anemones
feel the shiver of twilight at noon
hear the ancestors' distant cry
feel the ocean large and round
between his palms

let him cross some new bridges
make some new mistakes

and let him go

BODY UP

Rumi went to see god
who came to earth as the Guest
who is the ever-changing face
of the Beloved
and is the mother of all verse

and said, 'hey you, whatever-your-name
you who sit in judgement on mere mortals
and other lowly creatures
haven't you heard what the poet said
bodied, one will hunger
bodied, one will lie

if you don't know about this
or have forgotten
then try it for yourself
get yourself a body just like mine
flesh and bone, blood and guts

and see how you like it

BOOK THREE

EXTINCTION REBELLION

A TRIBUTE

We have just 12 years to make massive and unprecedented changes to global energy infrastructure to limit global warming to moderate levels, the United Nation's climate science body said in a monumental new report released Sunday.

"There is no documented historic precedent" for the action needed at this moment, the Intergovernmental Panel on Climate Change (IPCC) wrote in its 700-page report on the impacts of global warming of 2.7 degrees Fahrenheit, or 1.5 degrees Celsius.

From rising sea levels to more devastating droughts to more damaging storms, the report makes brutally clear that warming will make the world worse for us in the forms of famine, disease, economic tolls, and refugee crises.

vox.com

You must abandon poetry before it abandons you

Bill Manhire

LIVESONG

ANT AND EGGSHELL

the surface I walk upon
is a very pale blue
with tiny specks
where stars died

and it's curved too
rather beautifully

it's a structural miracle
the magic ovoid
in which movement quickens

everywhere I walk
is an unfolding horizon
always new

when I pause
it's to get my bearings
and when I turn my head to one side
it's to get a feel for the other
and the distant heartbeat of something
I can't even conceive

LIVESONG

it comes with certain mornings
before memory
in what the children call
the early world
when the light is diffused
in such a way
as to be
more fluid than shade

airy as a lover's touch
grazing the underside of a leaf
with pastels
slipping sideways
whispering through caverns of shadow
before birth, before time ticked
and the livesong was
everything that was
or needed to be
whilst the morning stands eternal
against light's passing

and the livesong lives on
wound through
the twilight of the living
and the dead

THEY

from here and there
and all over
everywhere
out of the woodwork
out of the shadows
out of the past
out of memory and desire
love and joy
delight and torment
and the mortality of angels

they creep forth
to gather
bearing a hard truth
still looking
for a home in the world

LIAR LIAR

liar, liar
pants on fire
nose as long as a
telephone wire

your brains aren't worth
a worn out tire

confess! confess!
to the great unholy mess

it's pretty dry now
and will soon be gettin' drier

TO A FRIEND IN BEIJING

living in a shroud
of soot
and filthy smudge
and desperate mirages

how can I write you
any kind of melody
as you can go for months
and never see a star
nor even a trace of the moon
but for a dull glow
overridden by neon and halogen
and rapid talk

there is so much noise
you are cut off from
the music of the spheres
those grand themes we find
in a whispering forest
or on the edge of a clean tide
or deep in the harmonies of ice

you must witness young children
coughing up their lungs
in sad hospitals
with sad windows
while the weather gets hotter
and the air begins to burn
with a chemical smell
and life becomes more and more
unlikely, impossible
conjectural
with everybody living for some
imagined future
or in some imagined past

it's a far cry, is it not, from how
we used to be, back in the day
when the sky ran open
and we did too
up the back roads and
along the river beds
you must remember
you have to remember

in the end
it comes down to language
the language of melody

the time signatures of forests and streams
children laughing in effervescent waters
the beat and metre of unfettered skies
cool air in the lungs
the contralto flash of a blackbird or a thrush
across an open window
the back beat
of trees green and dolphins blue
the clippings from bird song at dawn
or the sudden silence, the pause,
of a moment that becomes itself
and nothing more

if I were to write such a song
I might as well be writing of centaurs
and cyclopes, fauns and dryads
and three-headed dogs
and gypsy flowers
and fairy dust
for all its meaning to you
and what you see from your window

I might as well go hug a tree
and forget about all the rest

I can barely conceive what song must be like

for you, when all common referents
even the skies above and earth below
have been obliterated
and there are no spirits around
to make merry of the dawn
or streak your windows with sly colours
or a wind to touch your face with silk
how could I sing into your heart
or stir your spirit for the dance

let alone make you laugh
or cry

THE PATHOS OF POETRY

just in from India
a record breaking hurricane
a million people displaced

a struggle to put back a life
that will never be replaced

all over the globe, the same story

the dry gets drier, the wet wetter
oceans rip into coastlines
heat surges rip open oceans

I doubt these people
have much time for fancy lines

poetry can never become
the privilege of the protected
and the powerful
for it is always there, present
in the voiced grief and bitter hopes
of the survivors

GRIEVE WHILE YOU CAN FOR THE OLD MAGIC

grieve
for the mountains
and the sky
and the ocean
and all that is lost
and being lost
to us
as the old magic
drains from the land

turn wheel turn
how the fires burn

grieve
for all that lives and moves
and asks only to live
and move
with the larger movement
of the living and the breathing
as the old magic
fades
and death starts to stink
to high heaven

turn wheel turn
how the fires burn

grieve for paradise lost
even as your tears
dry up
and your cheeks crack open
and there's nothing left to drink
that doesn't stick in your craw

grieve for grief itself
as sorrow truly tragic
belongs to the old magic
to the catharsis of joy
but grief and its attendants
have fled
or been put behind bars
or sent to war

soon
there will be merely a hollow place
where grief once ruled
in all its trappings

and nobody will remember
what tears are for

LOST WORLD

trees that stood straight and tall
made a bid for the sky
and filled the air with scent
now lean drunkenly
or turn into ghosts that have
forgotten everything
except their mineral bones
and the stories their leaves once told
to the wind

bread that once nourished the blood
and gladdened the heart
now barely feeds the flesh
a promise hollow and empty

wine that warmed the belly
and staggered the mind
now smells of smoke
and tastes like an overripe sun
or vinegar tears

earth, that once basked
in its cool places

refreshing frosts
and shadowy dreams
now bakes or turns to slush

words, that once came crisp
and clean off the page
or from the hollow caverns
of the body
fade in the mouth, and choke
for want of space
to breathe

and for music we cannot say
for we have cast away
the original sound
from which all other sounds play
that note of grace

forfeited, and now hidden
the world we have lost

TEN YEARS

ten years to go
money to blow
nothing to show

ten short years long
we're all gone

pack the bong

THEY FIRST TO DIE

nobody gets it all
unless it's all there
to get

hard to put a planet
in your pocket
along with everything else

all that pride
takes up a lot of space

when it's all or nothing
the nothing is all
you end up
with empty pockets

and a planet that's not much use
to anybody
anymore

nobody gets it all
and some don't get any of it
they die first

AUTUMN

it's not yet as hot
as it could be
as it will be
as it has to be

we pop on our coats
we rub our hands
wipe some condensation
off the glass

the sun gets in a brief look
between showers

grateful we are
for that cool southerly wind

blowing off the ice

THE INTENTION

I'm in alpine territory
above the tree line
the last clump of birch

I can follow the intention
of the hills, all the way down
to distant green
or back up towards
the promise of snow

moss and rock cling
gravity glides
wind scars the slopes
the sky turns dark honey

there is no horizon
earth and sky just overlap
lips joined in open secrecy

I can lie down here, go soft
on the hard rock
and let the mountain do the dreaming

GEOLOGIC MOMENT: TONGARIRO

the lava flow broke off here
you can see
where the hillside
drops off sheer
to the folds of the valleys

you can stand at the very spot
where the blood tide of molten rock
oozed to a stop

we're in the land of mosses
lichens and liverworts

trees are a distant thought
and life is just something
that gets in under the fingernails

AS WE LIVED

our history will be written in rock
in the fossil records
in broken landscapes
and plastic filled oceans

the planet itself
will be our memorial
and our obituaries will be carved
from violent skies
and a shimmering heat haze

a short-lived species, as species go
for as we lived, we died

THE SENTRY

I've been standing watch
since the day it was announced
that our world was going to die
if we didn't stop
blowing each other up
mowing each other down
and heating up the air

there's no future in it
for the living or the dead

already my feet are strangers
to my mind
and I hardly know
who it is I'm watching out for
or why

everybody seems so normal

nobody looks like a criminal
or a mass murderer
and the barbarians all have suits
and revolving doors

my eyes grow opaque
and the dark is coming down
but there's no relief in sight
no echo of any footfall

no one else to keep watch
through the night

and no one to declare
a universal armistice

ANZAC DAY 2019

those guns have fallen silent
or at least fooled us into thinking so

the dead have stayed dead
or been very quiet about it

the land has repaired itself with flowers
or failed to do so

the mourners have gone back to their lives
or think they have

but, quite close by it seems
the war rumbles on regardless

MIMIC

we have it all wrong

it boasts a human body
feeds a beating heart
wears a human face

uses words that sound
just like ours

we mistake it for one of us
its camouflage is so perfect
nobody notices a thing

everybody wants in on the action
when there is a killing to be made
nobody hears the worm turn

when it takes off its face
we know it for what it is

we don't have to look twice

HOW WORSER

how bad does it have to get
we ask

from bad to badder
and worse than we ever imagined

the big heat and the big die off
the big hatred and the big pretend
isn't that bad enough

everyday we hide our faces
from each other
as it goes from bad to worse
and from worse to worser

still we ask
in as many voices as we can muster
how bad does it have to get?

IT DOESN'T BALANCE

the idea that everything balances out
in the end
doesn't balance out

supersymmetry is not so super

in fact, I'd say
things go out of whack
pretty damn quick

I'd like to think that these words
balance out the wordless

that there is a duet of night and day
a counterpoint of lines and spaces

that when someone is crying
someone else is laughing
but really, this is no laughing matter
and those carrying the burden
are running out of tears

I'd like to think
there is an even handedness
in the fall of a leaf
but the leaf just falls
and when the forest falls
the leaves all fall at the same time
revealing an empty sky

I'd like to join those who believe
that a great judgment will come down
upon the heads of the guilty
but it's just wishful thinking

I'd like to think of these things
as weighed on the scales
of some cosmic equity
but it really just doesn't balance out

and I'm feeling, way, way
way off center

BABY BOOMER SPEAKS

we are the ones who saw
our hopes for a better world
eaten away
to nothing
in the name of progress

not a better world
but a worse one
a worse one by far
beyond our dystopian imaginings

sister! how come we're all riding
the algorithms of doom?

brother, where have all
the pastures of plenty gone?

Oh mother
will ours be
The first of the last generations?

STILL WAITING

I've been waiting here
an eternity
for something to show

but that's about it
decency turns the other way

and by the time something shows
the show's over

the cosmos has turned
back into an egg
scrolls have rolled up the stars
rocks have surrendered their fire
and even late night footsteps
have turned for home

it doesn't pay to wait, pumpkin
it takes too damn long

SOFT BANDAGE

when a little gentle rain falls
we make amends

the first shall be last and the last
shall be first
we tell each other

it sounds good that way
a little green springs up
in our mind's eye
a little opening in the heart
to let the truth in
a soft bandage to the wound

we may not have the morrow
but we have the day
we tell ourselves

and the day has just begun

A NEW SYNDROME

I think I've got
hyper-stimulation-future-shock fatigue
it's a new syndrome
I just invented it
to explain how I'm feeling
and why my body is screwing up

I want to put my anchor down
in the real world
but I can't find it – the world I mean

the world that hides behind
all that jitteriness
and barely swallowed fear

I think the real world
is another false news story
but that just goes to show
so help me
what a grip this syndrome has
how deadly it can be
if not properly contained

and it's not getting any easier
to concentrate
with a mind that
slides off in all
directions
following will-o-wisps
into the galaxies of nowhere

there's no cure for
hyper-stimulation-future-shock fatigue
but it can be managed with the correct doses
of anti-inflammatory language
and love-peace-and-sisterhood

I don't know why it is that my pots and pans
turn into plots and plans
or why I get muddled with the sounds between
and find it hard to talk in the syntax
of common sense

things will only get more skittish and edgy
which is about the only thing
I can anticipate with any confidence

LINES RUNNING BACKWARDS

nothing
will come to

and all your projects, plans and policies
a world of vanishing futures
at least in this world
problem is, there may be no future
it all looks pretty good on paper
at least for you
when everything comes right
as we will be
it's all very well to imagine ourselves
if possible
for your children
and accumulating a little something
avoiding taxes
plotting and hatching schemes
to spend many hours
it's all very normal
everybody does
to make plans for the future
it's all very well

THE SAME WORLD

after the floods, everything grew
fast and rank

then

dried back, died back
and turned to tinder

each morning, we sniff the air
just to make sure
we're in the same world

OVERHEARD AT MT EDEN BUS STOP

too much of a good thing
is a bad thing
apparently

never thought I'd hear
anybody complain
about how nice the weather is
even this far into autumn

but there you go
no satisfying some people

hell, if it gets too hot
open a window

LET'S NOT PANIC

the climate's not changing
it's just the weather

sea levels are not rising
it's just erosion

the land is not drying out
it's just seasonal variation

a year's rain in one day
is a one in a hundred year event

and if I seem to be wrong
it's just because

everyone else is lying

CARTOON

the fat cat sits in the back
of his limo
and rolls up all his darkened windows

but he knows, he's seen the data
he's grasped the trend-lines
he's gone knuckle to knuckle with bar-graphs

he's faced what there is to face
he comprehends the nature of his ruin
as he has never comprehended anything
in his whole life

now he sees with uncluttered vision

with all the courage he can muster
he taps his driver on the shoulder
'drive over the cliff, James,' he says
'I'm committing suicide'

EXTINCTION REBELLION

her name is Blythe Pepino
she is a real person
a flesh and blood person
with flesh and blood hopes and dreams
who, against her deepest wishes
has decided not to have any children
because of "climate breakdown
and civilisation collapse"

my heart goes out to Blythe Pepino
and her partner
and their unborn children
whose lives are forfeit
before they are even conceived
to those who have too much
already

and if Blythe Pepino should wake one night
to the sound of a child crying for comfort
she should allow herself to grieve
and grieve wholly
for the generations of suffering
are coming to an end

GRETA THUNBERG

the child who cried wolf
got into a lot of trouble
when there was no wolf

the whole village got stirred up
all for nothing

the child is still in trouble
because the village is now crying 'no wolf'
when the wolf is obviously
at the gate

and only the child can see it

PROFIT AND LOSS

disaster capitalism will lead
to one final disaster
one ultimate market cataclysm

potential profits are staggering
but can never be realized

there's no future
to stack the futures up against

everybody else will go broke
and scratch in the ground
to grow potatoes
with one fearful eye
on the weather

BRAIN DAMAGE

some black snake has taken a bite
out of the moon

some maggoty hand
has taken hold of the earth

some bitter song
has crept into our throats

a dead humming noise
has taken over the night

a nameless stench
saturates the wind

twisted words
writhe on our screens

and we can't think straight
any
more

NEONICOTINOIDS

when bees die people die
it's not that hard to work out
Einstein had it figured

a combination of global heating
and neonicotinoids
with names like acetamiprid, clothianidin,
imidacloprid, nitenpyram, nithiazine,
thiacloprid and thiamethoxam
does the trick

marinate the environment in nicotine
then apply heat, wet or dry

the humble bees don't stand a chance
nor does much else

I'M WITH EXTINCTION REBELLION

why join the queues shuffling their way
to a passive death
like holocaust victims to the gas chambers

why watch the world die
for the privilege of the few
who know no shame
deny, defer, and denigrate
and then apportion blame

get a grip on yourself
join the young who refuse to die
quietly

sit down
sit down in front of the machine
stop the machine

let's bring everything to a great
grinding halt

let the traffic snarl
let the cops cop

let the judges judge
let the fools fool

let everything out
in one big shout

BACKDROP

the climate crisis
has now become the backdrop
to everything

all our dramas
all our personal stuff
all our precious
subjectivity

all our most wonderful
theories of everything
and intimate sense
of everything else

is going up in flames
or down in the flood

so why bother, you ask
why bother the already bothered

because that's what we do

when stuck on the end of a pin
we wriggle

THE TERRAFORMERS

they talk about going to Mars
Mars is the place to be
they don't have to

they are busy right now
turning Earth into Mars

RESPONSE TEAM

they were there
lines and lines of them
stretching into the distance

they came with their hands out
they came with their hearts sore
they came with their bodies broken

so we cut off their hands
ate their hearts
and buried their bodies
before they were properly dead

because we told ourselves
over and over
that we didn't care

AT YOUR DOOR

we are the lost ones
the missed ones
the disappeared
displaced

the harder you look
the less visible we are

the less visible we are
the more our presence is felt

the more our presence is felt
the more we are pushed
to one side

the more we are pushed
the closer we crowd

madness lies
just around the corner
where you will find us

staring right back at you

IT'S OFFICIAL

no, earth won't wink out of sight
caught in a wrinkle in time-space

it won't go up in a ball of flame
like a rag soused in oil

it won't go down to the roar
of the very last wave

people won't fall over dead
in the middle of the street

no god will appear
waving a big stick

in fact, we'll hardly notice a thing

and yet
we will have passed
that invisible mark in time
that final tipping point
the point of no return
beyond which

civilization becomes impossible
and humans will go down dying

looks so bald, just written down like that
with no frills, no supporting imagery
to comfort the mind
no turn into a supporting phrase
but we shouldn't be surprised
nearly every species that has ever existed
has become extinct
it's in the record
those crocodiles and cockroaches
are the exception that proves the rule

so by 2030
our doom will have become
inescapable
because we failed to act

but not much else will change
I expect
we'll have got used to the idea by then

MASSIVE HEIST

it is the most massive heist
the world has ever seen

a job of breathtaking scope
and daring

they stole the whole fucking planet

MUCH RATHER

I'd much rather do something else
like eat a strawberry

I'd much rather think about something else
like the girl next door

I'd much rather set my sights
on something nice
like a cool summer cruise to the Antarctic

I'd much rather love the love I love
than look around for another planet

I'd much rather have the time
to take the time, thank you
than be rushed off my feet
going nowhere fast

I'd much rather be
the idiot I am, than have to be wise
and see what I'd rather not see

I’d much rather sleep than have to wake
to another day in the slow death of life

I’d much rather write for the glory of god
than pen weather reports
for those who don’t read them

I’d much rather join the saints
than be a sock puppet covered in blood

I’d much rather celebrate
than have to bury the baby
in a cracked garden

I’d much rather be happy
than pack a sad

but here we are, where we are
and what we’d rather like

pretty much counts for jack shit

LESS SAID

the less said
the soonest mended?
I don't think so

take another look

WHO I AM

I’m pretty much stuck
with who I am and
where I am

and what I can divine

never thought it would go down this fast
or this hard

SEE YOU SOON SUCKER

I asked them to come around
to talk to me, comfort me
tell me this has all happened before
and every generation
becomes its own apocalypse

life goes on, the world keeps turning
no matter which way you look
and the poor will always be with you
the book says, which means
the empire will always be with us
and soldiers will never be far from the streets

but my ancestors have gone on holiday
maybe it got too hot for them, or they finally
got sick of the world
and my so-called spirit guides
are not much better, having, it seems
abdicated the field for fresher climes
and left me with a note that says
cultivate the self
or maybe it says, see you soon sucker

I don’t blame them for getting out in time
out of line, for their sorrow
for their pleading, for their profound
absence

because the dead need a living world
as much as we do

NO LONGER THE SUN

no longer those majestic
shafts of light you'll find
in the arched spaces of cathedrals
falling like a blessing
on the land and the people

no longer that zen glimpse
of a hidden garden
suffused with a soft glow
and damp vines of green
and sugary fruit

but rather
a terrible eye that never shuts
that levers open skies
where the light is always hard
and soft things wither away
and stones crack open
in dried river beds

a new sun has been born
pitiless, ferocious
the new god of refugees

DEUS-EX-MACHINA

once we could say, as a comforting truth
that while we lived and fought and died
and visited good and evil upon each other
all the rest would stand
                              that the sky
the ocean and the land
and all that may be evoked with our sacred breath
would be eternal
above and beyond our petty, murderous selves
always there to bring lilacs
to a broken land

that spring would come and creep through
the barbed wire, and autumn turn
deciduous forests into one swathe of
yellow and orange
and that winter fires light the heart

these comforts have gone

spring comes too early, too late
or not at all, summer turns autumn
into summer, forests turn into a swathe

of flame
while nothing is the same, sky
earth and sea
have joined the drama, not as backdrop
or as a Greek chorus
or even a character in a mask
but as *deus-ex-machina*
sweeping the action aside
in one great gesture

a solution to an intractable plot

CONSEQUENCES

we have played the game of consequences
and lost

we thought it didn't matter
we thought that there was more
where that come from
lots more

we didn't connect the dots
no matter how many
piled up

by that time we didn't give a rat's arse
about what lived and what died
as long as we hogged as much of it
as we could
before it was all gone

we turned our hearts to stone
and our souls to little wind up toys
that needed rewinding all the time
though propaganda and tricks
of the mind

we became incapable of perceiving
consequences and so
incapable of dealing with them

it’s very simple really
after a time, we just ran out of time
and the consequences
came rolling in

HUNG OUT TO DRY

as we neared the top of the hill
the sky regained its force
the earth embraced its own
delicious curve
and stars proclaimed their clarity

the world of us and them
and everyone else
fell away
just for a moment

you know
the way these things go

it all seemed
as if it were meant to be

when we got the top
it was all there
receding into thought and distance
landscape and memory

we went into a bit of a trance
we didn't say it, but it was
in front of us

a world hung out to dry

OF PENS AND SWORDS

in this situation, the pen
is hardly mightier than the sword
although it tries to be

we understand that all wars
are wars of the mind
sword or pen

the pen is double-edged
while the sword cannot cut the word
only air and flesh

and prayers may be heard
by the wrong gods

even if they are not spoken

SOMETHING ELSE

you can’t stop progress
they said

and that sounded right
even though it was wrong

and even when it turned out
to be something else
we still didn’t stop it

and kept calling it progress

THE SEDULOUS APE

like any kind of thought
it reaches saturation point

there's only so much
the monkey brain can take

confused by the consequences
forgetting the sequences
confusing the frequencies

we keep hitting ourselves
with the same rock, wondering
what's causing the pain
blaming god, or better still
the other guy

hell, we won't get far that way

better to empty the bucket
on the fire
than step in it

FORGET THE REST

from here on
it's nature that's calling the shots
not us, not our bots
we've shot our shots
we've shot the lot

no use pretending that geo-politics
lies at the heart of things
that's last century's game

the chessboard world
the rise and fall of politicians
the clash of ideologies
nationalist passions
and neo-con scams

now war and civil war are driven
by hot winds, dying lands
plague dreams
and the sudden floods that turn
into people

as crops fail

the water holes dry up
and babies wail

as the skies turn to glass
as the hurricanes make their landing

and cars bump and grind
down rivers of mud

it's pretty clear who is
and who isn't
in charge

PROVIDENCE

I don't see much providence
In the fall of a sparrow
or any other bird

I'm trying to take the larger view
that maybe when one garden withers
another flourishes
in an alternate time or space

I want to pretend
that there is some kind of even-handedness
in things
super-symmetry or whatever

humans may end their tenure
but earth must abide

except if it doesn't

there are dead and empty planets
aplenty
from gas giants to ice pebbles
to airless rocks

it wouldn't take much for earth
to join them
just a little push

a zombie planet, slipping through
the spacetime fabric
devoid of all but the memory
of something that stirred
in fresh winds

that there will be life beyond
the horizon of our instruments
as a matter of logic
is of little comfort

it's just buried somewhere in the mathematics
of enormous distances and
plunging time

I don't see much providence
In the fall of a planet

and a chance born out of miraculous odds
going nowhere

STEALING FLOWERS

whoever who stole flowers
out of time's garden
probably didn't know what they were doing
and ended up with wrinkled hands
failing eyes
and withered blooms

they just saw something bright
and beautiful
and reached out to touch
take
and break

one moment you're wandering along
with barely a care in the world
and a whistle in the air
next thing
you're carrying a bouquet of hours
still fresh
through the market place
where everything's for sale except a carefree
moment
and melodies are quickly forgotten

all those coveted flowers
will fade into the ancient faces of children
and miss their mark

HURTSVILLE

I've got a headache from all this
the heat, the mess
the betrayal, the kiss
the whole sick crew
the chemical stew

all this running back and forward
to the piss pot
all this over the top, take a shot
have a screw

the malevolence that chases clouds away
and fills the streams with didymo
to block them up and choke the flow

all this plays crazy with my mind
circles me, squares me, jokers me
drops me into evil dreams

this headache bores a hole
in my head, and everything else
get left unsaid

THE SMART MONEY'S ON TREES

plant as many trees as you
can lay your hands on, buddy

good hardy ones with a strong faith
a deep root system
and nice fat leaves

it's a good one to one-and-half degrees
cooler
in the shade
under the canopy
and it won't be long
before this kind of cover
is worth its weight

in gold

HEAT SPOTS

have you heard
there are heat waves
in the ocean

tsunamis of heat
turning the ocean
into a killing floor

you don't find
this kind of news
so easily
now the truth is out

it's too factual
it's too hard to spin
and can't be blamed
on Moslim terrorists
or eco-activists
or abortionists
or the Pope

have you heard?
have you heard?

spread the word

there are hot spots in the ocean
now
in which everything
dies

period

PRESS THE PANIC BUTTON

set the alarm
put a time limit on it

sleep is all very well, but
you can have too much of it

grief is all very well
but we have a surfeit of tears

anger is all very well
but there's been enough killing

set the alarm, and
sound the alarm

get yourself out of bed
take some deep breaths

let's do
what has to be done
quickly

EVOLUTION

if sharp claws survive
be a sharp claw

if it takes a mountain
to stay upright
be a mountain

show me the bird
that can build its nest in the air

show me the one that is
at one with the one
and I'll show you a world restored

if sharp claws don't do the trick
let them wither away

if the mountain can't take it
move the mountain

if it takes impossible love
then be impossible
and let's survive that way

AT LONG LAST

there comes a point
right now, in fact
when words leave off
and action begins

we've had enough words
already
fools talking backwards

if words don't lead to actions
they fester
ask any lover

when words fail us
we fail ourselves

all those grand plans
are little better than a scam

so tomorrow we hit the streets
not to march
but shut down the beast

extinction rebellion is on the move
pass the word

Deadsong

WHAT THE DEAD DREAM

the dead dream of forests
rushing silences
and cavernous streams

the living dream of red meat
warm sex
and money in the bank

those in-between haven't learned
to dream yet

they know only the haphazard winds
the slipshod stars
the hasty cosmos

and the echo of make believe

YOU AND I

you and I
we've seen our share of dawns
slipping between
the here and the there
the now and the then

you and I have had a fair go
you might say
done the rounds
shaken the sugar tree
stayed one step ahead of the sun

funny how slow
it's coming on this morning
bit by bit

I took a look outside myself
and hardly saw a glimmer
nothing that would lift the lid
on itself
and set itself free

it's not that we're waiting for anything

is it?

I've never seen a dawn yet
that held back
that could hold back
breaking day

you and I have to wonder, now
what happens next

THE KINGDOM OF DECEIT

we went over to the dark side
because the light got in the way

we hid our faces
when footsteps approached
we put our hands in our ears
when thunder clapped

some plausible, well-dressed people
told us we didn't have to think
for ourselves
or start connecting the dots
so we didn't
it was much easier that way
for a while

such a relief
to let other people
do all the thinking
for a while

if we covered out eyes
no one would see us

we thought

so we covered them
and the dark behind our eyes
was complete

if we cauterized our hearts
no one would hear them beating
we fervently believed

so we cauterized them
and the consolation was immediate

if we died quietly
we would enjoy a happy afterlife
we were assured

so we died quietly and here we are
with our apartment in the city of death

there was an answer to everything
and an answer to nothing
but we were too lazy to figure that one out
and besides
the drugs were really nice
and worked a wonder

so they stole our hands
our arms
our feet and our legs
our genitals
and our tongues

until there was nothing left of us
but chopped dreams
mass graveyards
and false memories

because that's what happens
on the dark side, in the land of slavery
in the kingdom of deceit

everything is offered
and everything is taken away
in the same moment

and freedom seems very far off

HEAT KILLS

the heat kills off the very young
and the very old first, they say

so being just born, I'm right
in the firing line
and being just dead, I remember it all
as it happened

in Aussie,
we have fruit cooking on the branch
from the inside out
neatly microwaved and ready to eat

bears falling out of trees
with bleeding eyes
birds falling out of the air
wings on fire
roads that twist 'n warp
fresh from a Salvador Dali painting

reservois that turn into cracked mud
dead animals that fall over
on their way to water

or lie clustered around a dry oasis
like a star made of bones

everywhere we look we see ourselves

really, I don't think I can make art
with these kinds of materials

I don't know why I'd want to
go there
but there you go

you work with what you've got
try to hold a mirror up to things
and then you find
that things are holding a mirror
up to a mirror

it's a hot day and promises to be
a hot night, restless and clammy

the heat, they say, kills off the young
and the old first, because their
inner thermostats don't work so good
and they can't regulate the blood
temperature

being one of the newly dead
it shouldn't affect me
however
this mind doesn't work
so good any more
and I can't be sure
if beauty is really truth
because the truth is no longer young

I keep up the good work anyway
as it's nice
to have something to do

IN THE FAST LANE

I had to go deep in
to where matter didn't matter
and was never matter anyway
so what the hell?

I had to go in
faster than the speed of light
faster than the speed of thought
past hologram projections
of multiple worlds
where people lived, unknowing
uncaring
past the two-faced judges
and half-faced gamblers
through all those mechanical dreams
and pokie machines
up and under
the other who was gunning for me
and down the other side
it was a helluva ride

until it all stopped one day
and I up and died

DEADSONG

it's no great shakes being dead
while walking among the living

the living have a living to make
the dead have a past to shake

nobody's got one up
on anybody else
except in their head

I'm sorry if you can hear me at night
pacing about
in solemn footfall, the heavy tread
it's just that I have fears to counter
and while it seems like
my death is a fake
I can hardly face the daily dread

It's all mixed up now
nobody came first or second
nobody won and everybody lost
and nobody knows how

children got old before they lived
the old stayed old too long
and there was never enough blood
to go around

it's no great shakes being dead
while walking among the living

I can only see myself
In the passing glass of shop windows
and can only see the world
in the frightened eyes of the living

these few gestures will have to pass
for motion and meaning
a feel for the whole and the part

for a stake in the world
that doesn't go through the heart

THE DEVIL'S WALKING PARODY

here in the afterworld,
I can wander with the dinosaur
the dodo and the mud-dragon
having lost it all
just like them

I reckon I've lost
what I never had
which is a funny feeling
like an extra limb that never was
or an eye that never learned
how to grow
or a wing that never knew
the art of feathers

fame and fortune pass by
from time to time
and all I do is tip my hat
to Wednesday
and carry on

they are always so busy
those twin sisters

with superior and important people
who seem, in hindsight
quite innocent of the nature of the world
how it comes and goes
tops and bottoms
and who gets shafted
in the end

love and affection come to visit
but I am never quite sure
when they will up and leave
with no goodbye
to look for another cave
in the mountains

I think I lost all the plots
except this one
(a mystery story, after all)
but I'm in good company
with all kinds of fantastic creatures
a bestiary of the outlandish
nature's genetic flings into the improbable
like wings too heavy to fly
or a carcass too big to feed
or a mind that lost control of greed

far too smart, but in the end
not smart enough

I feel quite at home
with nature's parodies
and I have no problem
when a bunch of dead
and ill-fitted birds
gather around to laugh at me

IT'S NOT WORTH DOING SOMETHING

dead men tell no tales
or so they say
but I wouldn't be too sure of that
I've heard a tale or two
from bare bones
and clacking teeth

mostly of daring
in the face of overwhelming odds

the stories the dead tell
are all cautionary by nature
none of them have the courage left
to propagate any lies
or bury the truth along with their bones

so
put your ear to the ground
and there's no telling what
you might hear
or read between the lines

they particularly want you
not to do what they did
the nature of which you may taste
in the particles of carrion
emerging from their mental cavities
like a host of ghost plagues
a visitation of funerals

but the dead tell tales all right
they'll speak out of turn
at every turn
steal the words right out of your mouth

they are total converts
to show don't tell
although a little show and tell
works just as well

stories arrive
from the deadlands beyond
the lowdown on the lowdown
the inside dope
what the dead say
when there's no one alive to hear

come! see the world

through our eyes for a while
go the extra mile
learn to smile
it's no good doing something

if it's not worthwhile

THE BOOK

the pages of the text
have blown away
or been stuck in the neck
of Molotov cocktails
soaked in accelerant

the paper was too thin
or
the words too frail
or
the glue came unstuck
or
everything just turned yellow
or
someone got the wrong
end of the stick

the binding was never designed
for the punishment
it is now taking

its pretentions look quite forlorn

and besides, the dead
don’t read too good

HANGED MAN AND THE TREE OF LIFE

I saw the nine worlds
devoured by flame
and dark

for nine days I hung
upside down
and watched the carnage
through alien eyes

the worlds cooked like fruit on a branch
the constellations began to glow
and then the great tree itself
even the tree from which I dangled
began to crack and lean
and deep in the rock its roots
began to quiver

in nine days everything which
had been made

was unmade

THE GRANITE BEAST

when I unwake
clouds are piled on my eyelids
pillars of fire address my wounds
and history is buried
in some far away music
beyond the horizon

my blood has turned to surging algorithms
my hands are fractal images
of each other
my arms bend like a stick refracted in water
my legs seek their own direction
in a river of stones

a neutron star pulses
in each eye socket
and I exhale through a straw
into the void
and from the void
back into the body of me
or me as body
so the rivers might flow
and the forests grow

slime-mould appears
from my spinal cord
and the air is filled with luminous
jellyfish, undulating
like fashion models on a submarine
catwalk

when I look around
people come up to me out of their lives
and want to know
what the hell is going on
who came first
and who hasn't been paid

I think I know but say nothing
in case I say what I don't mean
or mean what I can't say
and end up in a tango

some things are better left unsaid
especially
when talking to the dead

when I stand up, the world apes me
everything acts like
a mirror to everything else

so nothing shows
but the reflections
and the glimmer of a hidden
light source

words are backing up
nobody wants to go that far
beyond belief
beyond the pale

when I walk, nothing moves
in relation to me
as you might expect
my feet are giddy with stars
my knees go clink-clank
the machinery of my soul
will dip and glide

and when I speak, my voice
goes off like depth charges placed
many miles deep
where the ocean is most dense
and dreams are infinite

in the whispering whirlwinds
below the theatre of sound

words are forming and unforming
being and nothingness

when I unwake
the destroyer of forms
unwakes with me
and all hell breaks loose

GHOST STORY

as my foot hits the road
I can hear footfalls
echoing behind me

but I'm too scared
to turn around

especially as
those footfalls sound
just like mine

and there are enough of me here
already

I have to ask them to keep
to their own space and time
to keep their distance
and leave me alone in mine
but there's sweet chance of that
as with every step
those other steps
draw closer

NOT AS DEAD

you're never quite as dead
as you think you are

you cut into your flesh
with a razor blade

the relief is instant
you bleed

but the songs of the dead return
with bleak insistence
and there is nothing you can do
nowhere you can go
to make anything feel any better

as long as I draw breath
you say
as you draw another
and another

AMONG THE LIVING

at first
I was too terrified to move

I'd always had a fear
of being buried alive

I would dream of bells ringing
in misty churchyards at night
with no one to hear them

then I found I could move
only a little strangely
like action at a distance

and there was a world to move in
that somewhat resembled my own
air to breathe that almost tasted okay
and water that didn't

I could pass among the living
mostly unnoticed

I've heard a lot about the dead

not knowing they're dead
but from where I stand
it's the living who don't know
they're alive

FROM STREET TO WIND

1

I found a street
and walked along it

there were people doing
the things people do
when they're not doing
anything else

there was a dog, minding its own business
and a cat, keeping watch on the sky
and a tree with a sleeping bird

there was nothing to suggest
that anything was any different
so I didn't ask any questions

that worked until the end of the street
then there was another one

2

when I came to sit down

there were no chairs
so I sat in the middle of the air
like a saint in a Medieval painting

contemplating the worlds that spin
on the palm of god's hand
but seeing it all
from the wrong end of creation

what god won
is now undone
what he wove
is now unravelled
the roads spun
are no longer travelled

blame it on the ape that talks
the ape that learned how to think
but only got half way

when I got up to walk
I decided to keep
to the pathways of the sky
the gardens of the wind
the consolations of love
and the secrecies of water

to leave it all, seed and swarm
a world all torn
and find another place
to be born

3

when I came to pray
there was nothing I could say

no words to form
between formlessness
and form

no path
that wasn't too well worn

no gestures that would stay
no match between sound and sense

I had no knees to bend
no palms to clap
into a steeple
to bring the two halves of me
together

no tongue to shape the chant
that might grow in the heart
between beats

neither flesh nor feet
nor the spaces to move
from wind to street
to find a street and walk along it

YOU HAVE TO BE DEAD

you have to be dead to walk among
the homeless and the starving
over the garbage dumps
where children pick and fester
across beaches filthy with plastic
and trees that gesture to memory
from dry branches

well… you don't have to be dead
but it's easier

you fit in better
no so alone

feel right at home

BLOOD AND GUTS

it was a dark dark night
in a dark dark place
in the darkest of times

the vampires came out to play
blood enough to go round
moon enough to dance

where vampires dance
mirrors go still

there's nothing there but shades
it's all in our heads, they say
like a moon always full
like a song that never stops
a dawn that never comes

but while
the vampires have already
gone back to their coffins
cursing the light
we stay on to the end
still killing and spilling

more than enough blood to go round
more than enough moon
to dance

TRACERIES

looking back I can see
traces of a life
not much more

wasps and wisps

I could've made it up
or someone else could've
made it up for me

A TIME BEFORE THIS

before I died
I loved to take my fancies
for a ride
and to join them just for fun

before I died
there were worlds a-plenty
all dressed up
with words for every one

and everyone had their say

the horizon expanded and contracted
like an eye in the sky
and laughter did open commerce
with those close and far away

while children chased clouds
where clouds did fly

every stop was a start
every door was open,
every conversation a journey

every notebook entry
a tribute to an ongoing future
and every love
was a love for all time

then I died
and with heartbeat hung suspended

fancy fades
and so do I

THIS IS WHERE I DIED

If you like I can show you
where I died, the exact spot
the moment it came upon me
what I was thinking about
where my hands were placed
and what my feet were doing

even the expected is unexpected
when it happens
right out of the blue

all too soon
the world is at your door

I don't suppose, however
that geography matters much any more
even the dead want to move
to higher ground

I don't suppose the land remembers
beyond a certain point, or has to say
he died there
he was cleaning the car

and listening to the radio
some shock jock
ranting about the evils of immigrants

or she was talking on the cellphone
when worlds collided
and everybody jumped out of their skins

this, then, is where I died
right where you are
right where I said I would be

you can watch it for yourself
in real time
when the moment comes

A COMET'S TALE

I imagine this   continuity
but when I look there is none

the more I look the more
holes appear

the more gaps open out
between things

until there is nothing much left
but a comet's tail
and the mere memory of matter

DEADLAND

it's no bowl of cherries
over here in deadland
where the wind blows
hot and dry
from nowhere to nowhere
and seawater inundates
coastal springs
turning everything yellow
and the reservoir fractures
into a mud cake abstract

there're a lot of restless souls here
whose feet have lost the shape
of the earth
and whose faces have lost
the mask of the sky
the fit of the air
and whose minds will never be
the same again

over here in deadland
where blue has paled out of the sky
and the sun never goes away

and characters from past lives
chatter on about how things
used to be, back in the day
when they were alive
and still had a lot of loving to do
and summer green and blossom pink
would never leave the world that way
the slow fade
the desiccation of hopes

I'm sorry you had to wake up
and find yourself in this sort of company
in this sort of place
but it happens that way
you blink and the world goes away

and you're some place else
you never intended to be

THE LAMENT OF THE COLOURLESS

colours got drained away
hills faded
and cities turned grey

the ocean lost its blue
the air did too
and smiles were no longer scarlet

the green and yellows
went mellow
and then browned down

the mauves and purples
fawn, sepia and beige
apricot and magenta
everything with a nuanced shadow
dimmed
and washed right out

all that was vivid
turned livid
to look ashen was all the fashion

before you could say
show me the evidence
everything bleached into
grayscale
the tones of a stony riverbed
before turning inert, like lead

on the artist's palate memories swirl
into muddiness
the paint evaporates on the brush

so here we are at the gate, at the wall
hoards of us
with our grey faces and our grey eyes
and our shadowed lives
and our wan cries
up out of our earth graves
and sky graves
and the empty graves of grief

demanding our colours back

PROMETHEUS

I'm sorry to have to say
my mind is like a leaky boat
my feet are ablaze
my heart seems unprepared
for another day's hard labour
and I've lost my taste
for explanations offered
in soft voices

you might say I've seen better days

I don't have much to offer, I'm afraid
crows have been picking at my guts
harpies picking at my mind
while the rest of my body
keeps on saying hello to death
at the dawn of every day
always blood red

I can only dream of former glories
except there were no glories
all those stories were just made up
by unscrupulous poets

looking for someone to valourise
turning me into a figure
I could never be

they say I stole fire from the gods
to give to mankind
turning me into some kind of super hero
but that's a damned lie

mankind didn't need me
to do its dirty work

you'd been nursing that fire
in your breast
for a millennium
you mad monkeys

burning all that coal
was your own idea
not mine
but I have to carry it
for reasons that are deep and strange

those gods that men bleat about
have singled me out

I have my liver torn away each day
and the rock to which I'm bound
faces the incoming tide which is all fire and ice

with a bit of luck
I might just wriggle free
but I'm not holding my breath

I'm too busy screaming

THE HOUSES OF SLEEP

there are eyes that have never belonged
to the sky

faces that can't be found
in trees

feet that have never touched
the earth

bodies that have never known
the love of air

spider minds with no webs

aliens with no memory
of forests

while in the house of sleep
pillows gather dust

AFTERMATH

I roll to the edge of the bed
and look over

nothing but the abyss

the sheets are crawling off
the edge of dream

last night the talk
was all about love

the body next to me
is starting to smell

THE ROT SETS IN

after a while, tiredness creeps in
limbs get heavy
blood gets sluggish
and the mind doesn't mind

you can barely bring your eyes
up the horizon line

barely bring your heart
to the wailing wall

barely bring your mouth
to the river

the world, and all in it, slips
from your fingers

you want to say goodbye
but your words have forgotten
common courtesy

and your heart already belongs
elsewhere

MEMORY

the children play hop-scotch
jump and turn
through chalk squares

some can do it, some can't
some don't bother

the skipping girl comes by
wrists turning in a halo of rope
scattering the picnic

in a parallel world
none of this is happening
and the dead are content
to stay that way

WHEN THINKING BECAME TRUER THAN TRUTH

we were warned but paid no heed
we were told but didn't listen
(we thought we knew better)
the signs came and went
but we didn't see

we lost the words because
we threw them away
and when we needed them
scratched for them
we found they had been
spirited away

and suddenly everything
was in the past tense

time and again, it was pointed out
that if we didn't take action
we would lose everything
and we walked the other way

it was just cowardice, really
no wonder we are all, now,
just ghosts
wandering about in an afterlife
barely resembling the world

all the knowledge we needed
was at our fingertips
and we turned our backs
because thinking became truer
than truth

and in this way we lost our way

BACK IN THE BASEMENT

as the party parties
the shakers shake
and the pills are popped
and the air is filled
with the smell of forests

I can't help but think
of the vampire in the basement
and what will happen
when it gets loose

a drop or two of blood
in the cocktails
the fine spray of decay
in the air

I don't know, I must have taken
the wrong coloured pill

I can already hear the moans
and the bemoans
and all that vile sighing

one more hit

and I’m out of here

MONEY MAD

1

these big-shots and fat-cats
and know-alls and richy-bitches

are just cowards
when it comes to it

when it comes
to fronting up to it
fronting up to anything

they just run away and hide
and whine
for more of your money

2

nobody asks much anymore
where the money comes from

it's just money

but it can go on buying you out
until there's nothing left of you

and empty the world
before you can count your blessings

break the back of man or woman
or child
before they have stood upright

nobody asks much anymore
where the money comes from

but it would be better if we did

3

money!
money can fly with no wings
run with no legs
get rid of ghosts
perform
all kinds of magical tricks
to outsmart the gods

It's the best we have
this side of Christmas

get your hands
on as much as you can

while you can, buddy

it's said that you can't take it with you
but I don't know about that

I've seen a lot of dead people
on the move
with something jingling in their pockets

THE RETURNED

travelers from the future return
with tales of horror, war
and mass death

they are gagged and locked up
by the gaggers and lockers
the huggers and muggers

they don't like the idea of real history
or of people coming back
from the future
seeking a better death
and telling tales of chaos to come

they don't like the idea that their children
might come back to haunt them
as the hollow-eyed dead
so they do an angry stamping dance
and stamp on every face on which
the future is written

and frantically arm up
for horror, war, and mass death

ENDINGS

it used to be that you could steer your ship
by the whispered syllables of the stars
and weigh anchor
in the verses that lie snuggled
between peninsulas
and bays that smell of graveyards

you could find a safe place
between the lines
and the rhymes
of the road that leads over the hill
and around the coast
to the city of flowers
where the dead have made
a new life for themselves
in the provinces of plenty

that carefully stitched syntax
has come unravelled
because used-to-be arrived
reeking of nostalgia
like the yellow smell of broom
because the landscape

has abandoned poetry
for a life among the cinders
where there is no safe place
most of the feeling is done
in the past tense

and you can never trust
the endings
to deliver a true report

Also by Mike Johnson

Novels

Driftdead

Lethal Dose

Zombie in a Spacesuit

Hold My Teeth While I Teach You to Dance

Travesty

Counterpart

Stench

Dumbshow

Antibody Positive

Lear: The Shakespeare Company Plays Lear at Babylon

Shorter Fiction

Confessions of a Cockroach/Headstone

Back in the Day: Tales of NZ's Own Paradise Island

Foreigners

Poetry

Ladder With No Rungs, Illustrated by Leila Lees

Two Lines and a Garden, Illustrated by Leila Lees

To Beatrice: Where We Crossed the Line

Vertical Harp: The Selected Poems of Li He

Treasure Hunt

Standing Wave

From a Woman in Mt Eden Prison & Drawing Lessons
The Palanquin Ropes

Non-Fiction
Angel of Compassion

Children's Fiction
Kenni and the Roof Slide, Illustrated by Jennifer Rackham
Taniwha. Illustrated by Jennifer Rackham